AFRICAN CAMP-FIRE NIGHTS

N.B. AFRICAN BUFFALO TRAILS *is the abridged (and later) version
of HORNED DEATH; the more complete HORNED DEATH contains
five more chapters than the later version.*

AFRICAN
CAMP-FIRE
NIGHTS

by

John F. Burger

ILLUSTRATED

SAFARI PRESS, INC.

P.O. BOX 3095, Long Beach, CA 90803

CONTENTS

Chapter		Page
	Foreword	9
1	When Fortune Smiled	11
2	Lion Depravity	20
3	The Gentle Cannibals	27
4	A Date with Destiny	38
5	The Addict	47
6	In Dead Man's Country	61
7	Twice Lucky	72
8	Chiweta Tells his Story	79
9	Ronald, the White Mahuma	88
10	The Lion Again	101
11	The Ordeal by Poison	108
12	Akkabi Tells his Story	116
13	Echoes of the Past	126
14	Jumbos and Ju-jus	140
15	Killers in Action	151
16	Innocent Victims	163
17	Those Who Survived	170
18	Other Survivors	177
19	The Last Camp-fire	185

FOREWORD

I n this volume I have recorded some of the strange stories
I have listened to whilst sitting round the camp-fires at night
in many parts of Africa.

I maintain that the best hunters are not necessarily those who
are able to write interesting accounts of their adventures in the
bush. Few Europeans hunt for more than three or four months
in a year, and in those few months they often crowd in many
exciting adventures.

In the back blocks of Africa, hunting is a permanent and
necessary occupation with many of the native inhabitants, and
the conditions under which they hunt are vastly different from
those that apply in the case of European hunters who enter the
field with the most modern and reliable rifles and ammunition.

If the European, with all the advantages, still finds himself
in tight corners with the dangerous animals, how much more
so must the native who, in many cases, considers himself very
lucky to be possessed of an old antiquated blunderbuss, a spear,
or bow and arrow?

To the average European a close call with an elephant,
buffalo or lion is an adventure—something to write about. The
native, who is generally a fatalist in such matters, looks upon
it as a normal occurrence—an occupational risk—and it is rare
for them to capitalize on their adventures.

It is only due to the fact that I lived for so long in close daily
contact with these "men of silence" that I was able to compile
the notes in the diaries which I kept over the years. Some of
the stories I listened to often seemed incredible to me, but closer
investigation proved that they usually erred on the side of

modesty. Although I was not present to witness the incidents I have recorded in this volume, I have taken the greatest care to verify their authenticity.

JOHN F. BURGER

Pietermaritzburg,
Natal.

I

WHEN FORTUNE SMILED

Bill martin came to me just at the right time with a letter of recommendation from an old friend of mine. He was not only a good mechanic, so my friend said, but also a hunter with considerable experience. At the time I was due to start on a long safari to the Baluba country in the Belgian Congo, and some time previous to Bill's arrival I had passed the word among my friends that I needed a man with these qualifications.

It did not take long for Bill and me to settle the terms of the safari, and once on the way, I found that, in addition to the qualities mentioned in my friend's letter, Bill possessed another asset of great value, and that was moderation in speech. He was a man of few words—especially in regard to his previous experiences in the field, but he was always ready to discuss the current events of the day in an intelligent manner. Apart from mentioning to me casually that he had once accompanied Captain Sutherland, the well-known elephant hunter, on a safari in Northern Rhodesia, he hardly ever spoke of his past.

We had arrived at our camp the previous day, after considerable difficulty on a bad bush road, and when I was ready to leave with the hunting gang that morning Bill told me that he preferred to remain in camp to attend to the truck which required several adjustments after the gruelling journey through the swamps. That night as we sat round the camp-fire to discuss the day's events, there was more for us to talk about than usual, for earlier in the day we had had a stormy session with a wounded buffalo bull who had terminated his share in the excitement by tossing one of my porters. Before he could complete his work of destruction, and whilst he stood over the prostrate figure of the native, I had brought down the curtain on what would have been the next act in the tableau of "murder unlimited".

This unfortunate accident was responsible for the sombre atmosphere which prevailed as we sat discussing the sequence of events which led to the misfortune. Not far from us lay the injured native who was now busy giving loud vocal expression to his feelings. His injuries, although quite serious, were not nearly as bad as they might have been, for the bull had hooked his horn in a part of the sufferer's anatomy which would make sitting awkward for some time. For all that, the moaning and groaning, in which he was joined by his friends and brothers, helped to magnify the seriousness of the situation out of all proportion. It also served to revive an old argument which I thought we had long since flogged to death successfully.

During my wanderings in the bush I had previously seen quite a few accidents in the hunting field, some of them fatal and others only slightly less so. For the greater part, these accidents were caused by lions and buffaloes. My own experience had led me to the belief that the buffalo is the more dangerous of the two, but my old tracker, Ndege, who had been with me for many years, held just the opposite view. His judgement, I have no doubt, was greatly influenced by a nerve shattering experience he once had with the King of Beasts, a story he had told so often around the camp-fires that I felt certain I could repeat it, word for word, in my sleep.

"If that had been a lion instead of a buffalo, Kasembe would not be lying there moaning and groaning among his friends, he would be six feet underground by now," postulated Ndege.

"You are back again on that old saw, Ndege," I replied. "The trouble happened in open country and I could have shot a lion as easily as I did the buffalo, and before he could do any more damage than the bull did. Kasembe was lucky that he was hooked in the leg and not in the stomach or ribs, for if that had happened he would be cold and stiff by now."

"Oh, no, *bwana*, that's where you are wrong," he persisted, "a lion would not have stood over him like the buffalo did— he would have jumped on top of him and killed him before you could come to the rescue. When a lion knocks a man down he lies on top of him and tears him to pieces, and in that position you would not have been able to shoot from a distance of fifty yards without killing Kasembe as well. That bull was a fool, he stood there and waited for you to shoot him. A lion would never have given you that chance; I should know, didn't I . . ."

In order to avoid having to listen to a repetition of the same old story again, I cut the argument short by telling Ndege that if the situation ever arose and we were given the choice, I would pick the lion and leave him to deal with the buffalo.

It was at that stage that Bill entered the discussion. "In these questions," he said, "a person speaks in the light of his own experience. Personally, I have far more respect for a lion than I have for a buffalo, elephant or any other animal for that matter. Before giving you my reason for saying that I would like to show you something." Saying this, Bill pulled off his shirt and stripped to his waist. From the top of his shoulder, down to his waist-line, I counted no fewer than eleven enormous scars, whilst on the biceps of his right arm there were several others. After we had looked at the scars he continued: "A lion did that to me, and that is the reason why I hold him in such high respect."

Having got Bill so far, it was not difficult to persuade him to tell us the rest of his story, and he continued: "I was hunting on the Luangwa River in Northern Rhodesia when the head-man of a village some twenty miles away sent a runner to my camp and begged me to come to his aid and destroy a man-eating lion which was terrorizing the district. When I arrived at the village I was informed that the lion had not confined his attentions to the villagers only; in the course of a month he had taken several head of livestock in addition to three men. The other villages in the neighbourhood had suffered similarly and it was thought that the same lion was responsible for all the trouble. I agreed to try and destroy the marauder, and for four days we scoured the country looking for him but without success. During this time our meat supplies became seriously depleted as I had refused to shoot for the pot for fear that any indiscriminate shooting would frighten the lion away from the area. That night, before turning in, I had a long discussion with the hunting gang and it was decided that we would hunt for the pot the next day. But early the next morning we were back on the lion's trail with hopes running high, for during the night he had given plenty of evidence of his presence in the neighbourhood, having again raided a kraal shortly before midnight. By the time I arrived on the scene he had already departed with a goat.

"For the best part of an hour we walked in the direction he had gone, but he had apparently carried the goat in his jaws as there was no drag trail discernible. We searched the countryside until after 2 a.m., and as I had failed to pick up his eyes in the rays of my shooting lamp, I decided to return to my camp and get back on the trail with the first rays of dawn. Three hours later we were once again on the job. In the daylight it was much easier to follow the lion's tracks; I had Ammon and Wenda with me, two of the finest trackers to be found anywhere, and they had no difficulty in sticking to the trail. A few minutes after sunrise one of them came to the spot where the lion had devoured its prey. It was barely one hundred yards from the spot where we decided to turn back during the night. Had we walked that little distance farther I might have averted the disaster which was so soon to overtake me, for I would have been able to settle the score with the marauder very easily in the rays of a shooting lamp; under such conditions the lion is an easy target and quite a stupid beast, for he will stand and glare at the light long enough to give one time to take careful aim.

"The indications now were that the lion had vacated that spot only a few minutes before our arrival, and everyone, spotters and trackers alike, were on the *qui vive*. The surrounding country was fairly open with an isolated tree dotted at odd intervals, and visibility was good. Suddenly I was jerked by the shoulder; Jonas, one of my star spotters, had brought us to a halt and stood pointing at a big tree less than a hundred yards from us. Below the tree stood the lion, looking in our direction. We were below wind and this had helped us to approach so closely before the brute had picked up our scent or became aware of our presence. From his truculent stare it was quite obvious that man inspired no great fear in this devil, for he made no attempt to move and gave me plenty of time to line him up in the sights of my heavy .404 rifle. As he stood glowering at us I pressed the trigger, but it was at that same instant that he turned his head slightly. The resulting shot was clearly audible to us all as the bullet struck bone and the lion made a great leap in the air and promptly headed for a patch of grass which he entered before I could place a second shot.

"I was completely puzzled about the placing of my shot, for I had aimed for the neck and at such close range it was extremely unlikely that I had missed the target. There was also the tell-tale thud of the bullet when it struck home. With a heavy calibre .404 soft-nose bullet in his neck or head, the lion should have dropped dead on the spot. His wild leap and the speed at which he entered the grass, however, indicated that he had suffered no crippling injury. It was a strange and puzzling development for which I could find no ready explanation.

"The patch of grass which now provided the lion's cover did not measure much more than seventy-five yards at the widest point. Beyond that there was more open country on a sharp upward slope. I immediately called in the spotters, trackers and porters and we cautiously advanced in the direction of the grass patch. When only fifty yards separated us from the spot where the lion had entered the grass, I signalled for the natives to halt, and for a minute or two we stood looking in the direction the lion had gone. It was one of those tricky situations in lion hunting which one has to face on occasions and take weighty decisions. The trail showed distinctly that the lion was losing a lot of blood. To enter the grass with a wounded lion at bay would have been the height of folly, but to allow him to escape unnoticed was not part of my plan either.

"I was standing turning the situation over in my mind when the spotter beside me tapped me on the shoulder and shouted *'hapa bwana hapa'*, at the same time pointing at the open space on the far side of the grass. And there, trotting at a moderate pace, was a big black-mane lion. As I raised my rifle to my shoulder he suddenly came to a stop, turned round and glared at us. It was a superb target at a range of little more than a hundred yards. The lion was standing on an elevation with its head raised high and the entire chest well exposed. When I pressed the trigger I knew that the shot would be well placed in the throat as I intended. When the lion went down in a heap as the bullet struck him, I had no doubt whatever that he was dead. The natives were wildly excited and had already started running towards the kill when I called them back. For fully five minutes we all stood watching the lion intently. Apart from a dying kick or two, there was no other movement. Still, I was not quite satisfied, and before entering the long grass to cross over to the kill I instructed trackers to remain on the spot and watch the lion closely. If he should show any signs of life whilst I was in the grass they were to shout and warn me immediately.

"With all these precautions, and a feeling of certainty that the lion was dead, I held my rifle at the ready and entered the grass. I had hardly walked twenty paces when it happened—a savage snarl and I found myself lying on the ground. A second later the brute was on top of me trying to sink his fangs into my shoulder. There was a sharp pain as the teeth fastened into my flesh, but I could not hear or feel the crunching of bone which I thought would be inevitable. All this time the lion was snarling viciously and there was a deafening roar in my ears as he gave vent to a series of loud, menacing grunts. The pain in my shoulder became unbearable but still the lion was not pulling me to pieces as I expected him to do. For a moment I felt that if I could only hold him off for a little longer I might be able to save myself, for in my belt on my left side was a fully loaded revolver, but my arm was pinned under the brute and I could not move it. Now he began moving his jaw towards my throat and the foul smell of his breath started to suffocate me. From his wide-open mouth the blood was pouring rapidly all over my face and chest. Instinctively I put out my arm to protect my face. In a fraction of a second the huge jaw closed over my arm. Again there was no crunching of bones as the jaw closed—all I could feel was the terrific pressure of the upper jaw when the fangs pierced my arm.

"It was at that moment that I noticed the bottom jaw almost completely torn away. The mystery of the bullet striking bone without giving any apparent results was fully explained. As the bullet tore through the lower jaw it had completely shattered all the bone. Large portions of the tongue and jaw were completely missing and this explained why he was not able to inflict more serious damage. But for all that, I was still in a most critical dangerous position.

"Once again the brute attacked my shoulder and I could feel the burning pain as the fangs of the upper jaw entered my flesh. I lashed out with my fist and the jaws immediately moved towards my throat. As I put up my arm for protection and pushed back the head, I again looked into the gaping mouth with stubs of bone protruding from the fractured jaw. It was a horrible, sickening spectacle.

"But now the weight of the brute and the nauseating stench from the wide-open bleeding mouth began to overpower me. The last recollection I had was the jaw once again closing over my arm, after that all went black. When I woke again it was from the effects of cold water being poured over my face. The natives had carried me to the shade of the tree from where I had fired the shot and brought me back to life by emptying their water bottles over me. There was an excruciating pain in my right shoulder and a dozen open gaping fang wounds. The pain was such that I could not move my arm and it was not possible for me to tell whether any bones were fractured. Another futile attempt to move my arm brought on a further spell of unconsciousness, and when I awoke again two hours later it was to find myself in a *masheila* with a gang of natives travelling at top speed to Fort Jameson hospital. There I lay in agonizing pain for two weeks but I was conscious for only part of the time. It was quite a year later before I could use my arm properly again.

"When I was on my way to recovery I was told by my trackers what happened after I had fainted for the last time under the lion that day. Both trackers had immediately come to my rescue when they heard the lion roaring during the fight, but the brute was lying on top of me and they were afraid to approach too closely to shoot him. It was Ammon who eventually came close enough to hold the rifle at an angle that would not endanger my own safety and pulled the trigger to kill the lion. Of all that I luckily knew nothing, as I was out for the count.

"How did the accident happen? In the bush the best laid schemes are liable to go wrong. The other lion which I had fired at on the far side of the grass and saw go down, was dead without any doubt at all. But how was I to know that he was the mate of the one I had fired at first and that the wounded one was lying in the grass waiting for me? It was the kind of accident that could have happened to the best and most experienced hunter. I was lucky that my trackers did not abandon me to my fate that day. It needed a lot of courage to crawl within five feet of an enraged lion—and it must be remembered they did not know at the time that the lion's jaw was shattered. At all events, you will understand now why I hold the lion in such high respect."

Ndege was quick to resume the argument about the respective danger of the two killers. "You see, *bwana,* how many hundreds of buffaloes have you killed and how many have charged you and come off second best. Not one has ever been able to do you any harm. The lion is the most dangerous by far, I should know, didn't I . . ."

I could of course have pointed out that, under similar circumstances Bill might have fared much worse if he had to deal with a leopard that day, for the spotted cats use their claws far more effectively than does the lion. Also, if a buffalo bull had filled the role in the grass that day the results might have been very different. But each man is entitled to his own opinion in this matter; the main thing to remember is that each and every one of the killers is capable of bringing down the curtain for the grand finale if the conditions are right.

2

LION DEPRAVITY

Lion cubs are born with their eyes only partly open. During the first eight or ten days their vision is extremely poor. For the first three months their sole nourishment is milk. At the end of three months they are weaned and the mother then brings them portions of meat from the daily hunt—often she will regurgitate for their benefit. At this stage of their development the mother is extremely hostile and aggressive, and as in the case of dogs, her main concern in life is the welfare and protection of her cubs. A few months after the weaning period is over and when they have gained sufficient strength, she will permit them to accompany her on her daily outings in search of food. This is where the "education period" starts.

The education part of the business is one of the most gruesome and merciless features of animal life in the forest, for, in order to give the cubs the right slant on the killing and devouring side of the game, mother lion will often pull down her prey and hold it down whilst the cubs devour the victim alive—piece by piece.

This dissertation on lion conduct is necessary so that readers who are not conversant with their habits may more easily understand the behaviour of the lioness in the present case.

Lion hunting, as such, has never appealed to me in the same manner as it does to the average collector of trophies and seekers of thrills and excitement. Most of my encounters with the King of Beasts were due to the fact that when on occasion I happened to be in a district where lions were troublesome and resorted to man-eating or the raiding of livestock, I have always been willing to lend a hand and bring the culprits to book.

When I was hunting in the Rungwa district of Tanganyika Territory, my interest, as usual, was confined mainly to buffaloes and not to lions. For a change, my luck held good on this safari, for the lions in this district were all on their best behaviour and the natives in the different villages we visited had no occasion to appeal to me for help. But if the safari did not present me with the opportunity, or necessity, to cross swords with the King of Beasts, it nevertheless afforded me the opportunity of listening to one of the most gruesome stories of lion depravity I had ever heard in all my years of hunting. And not only did I listen to the story, but all the evidence was there to prove its veracity, for the teller was no other than the victim himself.

When I entered this particular area in the Rungwa district I frequently listened to stories about a famous native hunter by the name of Fundi Mtatu, which, in the Swahili language, means "three hunters". In the present case it denoted a man whose capacity as a hunter equalled the ability of three men. In these parts it is not unusual to hear stories about natives who had survived a mauling from a lion; such incidents often happen during hunts or when they take up arms against man-eaters or marauders. Thus, when the natives sat around the camp-fire that night and told of Fundi Mtatu's miraculous escape from a lioness I did not attach any undue importance to the story. But now I had arrived in the vicinity of the village where Fundi Mtatu was the headman and late that afternoon we pitched camp a few hundred yards from his kraal.

When a European hunter camps near a native village it is customary for the headman and several of his followers to come forward to pay their respects and offer assistance in the matter of guides and porters. Shortly after we had settled down a number of villagers appeared on the scene. They were all

anxious to join in the hunting and offered to show me the best
game haunts. When I inquired from my visitors which of them
was Fundi Mtatu I was told that he was not present for he was
at that moment busy settling a serious matrimonial dispute. He
had, however, asked them to tell me that he would call on me
later in the evening after he had settled his trouble at home.

It was whilst we were sitting around the camp-fire that evening with the hunting gang all busy grilling their meat over the
fire that Fundi Mtatu appeared on the scene. He was an elderly
man who walked with the help of two crutches for he had only
one leg and his left arm was completely distorted. For all that,
he was a pleasant person and readily accepted my invitation to
be seated near the fire. After he had taken up his position on a
log beside me I instructed the cook to bring him a generous
portion of the meat of a roan antelope I had shot earlier in the
day. I offered him a helping of tobacco, and after he had filled
his pipe the discussion turned to hunting and the prospects of
finding something worth while in his part of the country. I was
naturally anxious to hear all about his adventure with the
lioness and as he had failed to mention the subject I asked him
to tell me the story.

"Oh, that is a very bad story, *bwana*, a very bad story indeed,
but it will take a long time to tell, perhaps we can leave it for
another time?"

I was determined not to miss the opportunity of listening to
his story, and another fill of tobacco, accompanied by a stiff
tot of brandy, had the desired result.

"It happened early one morning, *bwana*. The lion had raided
our kraal the previous night and carried off a young calf. Before
sunrise that morning I called out six hunters, including my son,
to accompany me on the trail. We were all armed with spears
and hippo hide shields and I also carried my gun (an old
muzzle-loader). We searched around the kraal for tracks but
found none, nor did we find the place where the lion had eaten

the calf. We were walking towards a hill, not far from the village, about twenty yards between each of us. It was as I entered a patch of dry grass when it happened.

"The lioness jumped on me unexpectedly, my rifle and spears were knocked from my hands and I fell to the ground and shouted loudly. The lioness snarled and growled viciously and then picked me up in her jaws and started to carry me off. I was still dazed from the blow she had struck me when she knocked me down, but my mind began to clear and I pulled my hunting knife from my belt and stuck it into her side. As the knife entered her side she growled in a terrible voice and fastened her fangs deep in my shoulder. The pain was so terrible that I was unable to think clearly for a while. She was trotting at a fast pace and my feet were dragging beside her on the ground. As soon as my mind cleared a bit I again stuck the knife into her side. This must have made her very angry for she roared even louder than before and she bit much deeper into my shoulder. I could hear the bones cracking and began to feel faint. A moment later I lost consciousness and I did not wake up again until she dropped me near a cluster of dense bushes.

"Almost at the same moment her two cubs came rushing out of the bush and the larger one, which must have been a male, jumped on top of me and started to tear the flesh from my leg. I still had the knife in my hand, it was hanging on a loop through which I had pushed my forearm before I dug it into the lioness. I struck the cub a blow with all my might and that sent him away yelping. At that moment the mother snarled loudly, picked me up in her jaws and shook me like a cat shakes a mouse. Then she dropped me and lay across my chest. Both my arms were pinned to the ground and I could not move. The cubs must have known that I could not hurt them for they now both started to tear the flesh from my leg. Each time they tore a piece of flesh they grunted viciously. I began to pray that I might die quickly, for I could feel them chewing at my flesh higher and higher up my leg. It was a terrible thing to lie there helpless and know that you are being eaten alive.

"I screamed loudly but neither the lioness nor the cubs took the slightest notice of me. The lioness lay over my chest whilst the cubs were feeding, but she took no notice at all, she had her eyes fixed on something in the distance and kept on purring and grunting. By this time the cubs were tearing the flesh from my leg high above my knee and I began to feel weak. I tried to shout again but no sound came from my throat and then everything went black.

"When I awakened again I was back in my hut and all my people were crying and wailing. They had tied a string round my leg to stop the blood and they were washing the wounds with hot water. When I looked at my leg I could see that all the flesh was eaten from the bone for quite a foot above my knee. I knew then that I must die, for the wounds were bleeding rapidly in spite of the string they had tied round my leg and the pain was so bad I could not bear it. I was closing my eyes and preparing to die when we heard a car stop outside my hut. I cannot remember what happened to me after that, for when I awakened again I was in the hospital and there was a European doctor standing over me. I learned afterwards that it was the district medical officer who stopped outside my hut that day and took me to hospital where they amputated my leg and re-set my shoulder. But I was too ill for a long time to worry about anything. It was a long time afterwards when the doctor came in one morning and told me that they would have to amputate again as some of the wounds would not heal and had turned septic. I remained in the hospital for more than a year and I left it in the condition you see me now. The wounds have healed but I am never really free from pain, and when there is rain about I suffer a great deal. But I am not complaining about that. I was lucky that I did not lose my life. That is the story, *bwana*, it is a very bad one, is it not?"

"Yes, Fundi Mtatu," I agreed. "It is a terrible story but you have not told me all of it. You have not explained how you managed to get back to your hut and what prevented the lions from killing you and eating you."

"Of that I can remember nothing, for I have already told you that all went black until I woke up in my hut. But my son over there was one of our hunting party that day; he can tell you the rest."

The son, Mabunda, now took up the story. "When I heard my father calling out that day I was about fifty yards from him and I immediately rushed over to see what the trouble was. When I got to the spot from where I thought the cries came I found no sign of my father. I started looking round for tracks and called out loudly but there was no answer. Then I found the spot where the trouble had occurred, it was easy for me to read the signs on the ground. I shouted for the other hunters and they quickly joined me. We then followed the trail of the lioness. It was not difficult for we could easily see the drag marks on the grass. When we came near the spot where the lion had taken my father we could hear the grunting and growling. We crept up cautiously without attracting the lioness's attention, for the wind was blowing towards us and in this way we kept under cover until we were quite close to her. When we looked over the cluster of bush behind which we had taken cover we could see the two cubs tearing the flesh from my father and swallowing it.

"We realized that there was no time to lose, and with our shields fixed to our arms and our spears in hand we rushed forward. The lioness was taken completely by surprise, for the noise the cubs were making must have prevented her from hearing us until we were almost on top of her, and before she could attack we threw six spears into her. But that did not kill her for she came out in a great rush and knocked down one of our men. Before she could attack him we put five more spears into her and this time she rolled over dead. We then rushed up to my father; the two cubs were still busy tearing away at his leg and we quickly speared them.

"After that we carried my father home which, luckily, was not far away. The rest you know. But it is sad to think that all this trouble could have been avoided if we had looked more carefully for tracks near the village that morning before we left on the trail that led us to the lioness. She had nothing to do with the killing of the calf that night. It was a big male that was responsible, for we found part of the remains of the calf later in a totally different direction. That lion was later killed by two Europeans who came out to the village and sat up at night waiting for him."

Fundi Mtatu, who had been sitting listening to his son, now stirred himself. "There is rain in the air I am sure, for my leg is aching very badly and it will be well for me to return home." The sky was clear when Fundi Mtatu took his leave, but by three o'clock the next morning our camp was drenched in a terrific downpour.

3

THE GENTLE CANNIBALS

My meeting with Pierre Delmont at the little village of Adranga near the Uganda border was quite fortuitous. I was at the time heading for Uganda after a hectic trip through the cannibal country of Ubangi. Pierre had been much farther afield, for he was returning to the Belgian Congo after a lengthy sojourn on the Ivory Coast and in French Equatorial Africa. I had not previously visited the Ivory Coast and knew nothing about conditions there.

As I intended to cross over to Uganda at a place called Arua and Pierre was on his way to Lake Albert, we decided to join safaris on our way south. It was as we sat round the camp-fire that night after our first day's trek that I told him about some of the nerve-wrecking experiences I had had on my trip through the Ubangi. He sat listening to my account with obvious interest, and after I had told him the gruesome story of three men whom I had found in a river, tied together, with their arms and legs fractured—the cannibal method of softening up the flesh before the victims are killed—he remarked, "Your cannibals of the Ubangi are a savage crowd and I should hate to have any dealings with them. On the Ivory Coast they are a fine, gentlemanly lot, and although I saw and learned quite a good deal about them and their methods, I certainly never felt insecure amongst them, and that goes also for the time I spent amongst the witch-doctors and sorcerers of which there are a great many on the Ivory Coast—all comparatively cultured and respected people. I lived amongst them for the best part of a year, and apart from the fact that I never wilfully resorted to man-eating, which is a regular practice with them, I was looked upon as one of their own after I had taken the precaution of becoming an initiate in several of their minor cults and got myself on good terms with their many gods, fetishes and oracles. Some of the things I saw done in the forest are so astonishing as to be almost incredible.

"I first formed the idea of travelling through the interior of the Ivory Coast after I had worked as a civilian in Cape Palmas for about six months. During that time I frequently listened to the most fantastic stories about life in the interior. Once I had made up my mind to undertake this journey I devoted every minute of my spare time to gathering all the information I could from both Europeans and natives, and most of my earnings were put aside to finance the trip. It was nearly twelve months later when I set out for the Sassandra River. My safari consisted of some thirty porters, each of whom carried a 65-lb. load. For the greater part the loads contained trinkets—beads, cheap jewellery, cloth, pocket knives, rock salt, mirrors, etc. We also had a good supply of canned food and rations for myself and my native porters. In addition to the porters, I took with me a cook and an interpreter of the Yafouba tribe. He spoke French fluently and had spent the greater part of his life in the Yafouba country.

"At first the journey was uneventful, but when we reached Soubré, on the Sassandra River, Yafu, my interpreter, informed me that we could not proceed farther without first consulting the local witch-doctor who would give us the necessary instructions in regard to the different rites to be observed on our way through the forest—instructions which had to be scrupulously observed until we reached Guiglo where another witch-doctor would give us further advice and instructions. In short, I was to become an initiate and not only respect, but participate in many of the mysterious rites of the Yafouba tribe or abandon all thought of passing through the country in safety.

"That night I was presented to the village sorcerer, an old man who sat in an ill-lit hut, the walls of which were adorned with a vast collection of human skulls. After I was ushered into his presence I was invited to be seated on a floor mat beside him, and for several minutes the old man sat in silent contemplation, gazing in turn upon each of the skulls on the walls. It was an eerie and macabre performance which lasted for fully half an hour, after which the sorcerer called for Yafu to enter and explain to me the different rites the oracle had prescribed for me to fulfil in order to propitiate the many gods who controlled that part of the forest through which I intended to travel. And there were many gods indeed—the god of the forest, of the air, of the trees, of the water, of the lightning, and so on, and each had to be appeased in some prescribed manner. The god of the ground, for instance, would be pacified if I walked barefooted for a certain distance at an indicated spot, take a handful of earth which my bare feet had touched and wrap it up carefully and hand it to the next sorcerer, who would sew it up in a bag which I was to carry with me for protection against evils that may arise from the ground.

"There were also definite rules to be observed in respect of the other gods, and the oracle had indicated that it would be necessary for me to enlist the support of a lesser sorcerer to accompany me on my journey. He would instruct me in the matter of procedure along the way, for there were villages where it would be dangerous for me to accept food or water from inhabitants. In others again I might do so without evil resulting. Similarly, there were other villages where the offer of any gift had to be preceded by certain rites such as having the blood of a freshly killed chicken or goat rubbed on my hands and on the package from which the gift was taken. At this village, in accordance with the command of the oracle, all my porters had to be replaced by local men. The rate of pay for a porter in those parts is about a penny per day, plus his food, which, as in every other part of Africa, consists of meal and meat. The latter I supplied in large quantities as game was plentiful and I was well equipped with rifles and ammunition.

"From this village onwards we travelled through a land of mystery, superstition and fear of the unknown, a land of a million fetishes in which the witch-doctor, under the guidance of oracles, ruled supreme. At many points on the track we followed there were long poles planted on each side with crossbeams from which hung numerous skulls, all decorated with beads and other ornaments. There were many small paths which turned off at right-angles and led into the forest. These paths were curtained off by reeds through which only witch-doctors of a certain standing were permitted to pass. These paths, I was informed, led to secret places where sacred rites were performed and which the uninitiated were not permitted to witness. Along the sides of the main forest track there were numerous idols—human skulls, bones, wooden images, sacred stones, etc., all draped with cloth and beads. These idols are completely inviolate and death is the penalty for anyone who dared to touch them. On several occasions when we became aware of the presence of Leopard Men, the terror and scourge of the forest, we camped at night near an idol and felt quite safe, for even these savage marauders have a wholesome respect for the spirits and would not dare to violate that ground.

"The apprentice sorcerer who accompanied me on this part of the journey must have been well advanced in his profession. The forest was an open book to him; he was well known and exercised a marked authority over the inhabitants of the different villages through which we passed. In one village where we spent a few days a great welcome awaited us. This village was controlled by yet another sorcerer of apparently higher standing than the one who accompanied me. He had arranged a special entertainment for our benefit. This entertainment consisted mainly of strange dances and invocations, including the exorcizing of evil spirits. The star turn was a demonstration by snake charmers who performed without the aid of music. The snakes, large cobras, were held up for my inspection and I found the fangs all intact, but whether the poison ducts had been removed I could not tell. The head performer allowed the reptile to crawl all over his body and finished up with the snake's head in his mouth. It was all very impressive but I did not think there was anything that called for supernatural intervention. I was, however, informed that the witch-doctor at the next station I was to visit was much more advanced and that he would stage a performance for me by the most renowned of forest artists—the sword jugglers. These men, I was told, performed whilst under the complete control and influence of the witch-doctor. The nature of the performance was explained to me by my interpreter, who had often seen it before, and left me with cause for serious reflection. He explained that the performance could not be accomplished without a dexterity not likely to be attained by a raw native in the bush. It was quite a week later before we reached this village and I was presented to the head sorcerer. I was invited to enter his hut where once again I was anointed, this time with fresh blood from a goat. Incisions were then made in my arm and also on the doctor's, and the blood mixed and rubbed on our respective foreheads. This ritual, I was told, raised me to a higher standard among the order of initiates. The fact that I had scrupulously followed the prescribed formalities along the road had qualified me for this distinction and I was now accepted as a member of their order. The entertainment would be staged the next afternoon in order to celebrate the occasion. The oracle had been consulted and his sanction obtained for the sword jugglers to perform.

"The next day there was an amazing exhibition of dancing accompanied by the usual invocations, and then the stage was set for the main act of the afternoon. From a nearby hut emerged two powerful men, stripped naked but for a loin cloth. On their faces long white lines were painted which extended to their shoulders, and they wore hideous masks. The two men advanced to within a few feet from the sorcerer and bowed low, their heads all but touching the ground, whilst the doctor enunciated a series of weird chants and more invocations. At his word of command they withdrew to the centre of the enclosure not more than five yards from us and around which hundreds of villagers had gathered. A moment later two naked baby girls were led from another hut and they too bowed before the old man, and the same performance was repeated as in the case of the two men. At the end of the invocation the girls were ordered to rise and stare in the face of the sorcerer. It was obvious that he was exercising hypnotic influence over them and a few moments later they both rolled over and curled up on the ground. The jugglers now approached and lifted the two girls in their arms and returned to the centre of the enclosure where they took up their positions, ten feet apart, and in true juggler fashion, the two unconscious forms were thrown from one man to another. Towards the concluding stages the bodies were thrown fully ten feet high and caught gracefully by the performers.

"Now the juggler at one end laid the unconscious form on a mat beside him whilst the sorcerer walked up and presented him with two swords which he firmly fixed points upwards in the ground before him. The same performance was repeated at the other end. At a signal from the sorcerer a body came hurtling through space, and from a height of fully ten feet the unconscious child landed on the two upturned points with a sickening thud. The same performance was repeated at the opposite end and for fully two minutes I sat looking at the two forms suspended in space on the points of the swords. At this stage the old man walked to a point half-way between the two men, knelt down and uttered more invocations and signalled for the jugglers to continue. The swords were lowered and both girls gathered in the arms of the man beside her. At that moment the spell was broken and both girls showed signs of life and started talking to the men holding them. They were lowered to the ground and immediately walked to the seat which I occupied beside the witch-doctor. I forthwith examined both girls carefully—there was not a mark or a spot of blood to be seen on either of them.

"This astonishing act was performed in broad daylight not more than five paces from me. That both girls landed on the points of the upturned swords is quite certain. For the rest I am unable to offer any explanation. I have previously seen hunters in some parts of the Congo kill lions single handed by goading them into an attack and hold their spears in such a manner that the lion will jump on to the upraised point. It is very rare for them to fail and in almost every case the lion is impaled and rendered harmless or killed instantly. The performance I had witnessed here was, to all intents and purposes, identical, but neither child was harmed in any way. How was it done? I have pondered over it for many many hours and failed to find an explanation.

"I was even more puzzled when the witch-doctor informed me that on occasions when the oracle had given his sanction the girls were transfixed on the swords and carried round the enclosure with the points protruding from their bodies. On this occasion the oracle had refused to sanction such a performance and without the necessary sanction the act would be too dangerous. Whether this is true or not I do not know, but the statement was well vouched for by several of the elders and also by my interpreter who stated that he had seen the act performed on a number of occasions. This was only one of many strange and inexplicable things I saw done by the witch-doctors in those parts. Equally baffling is the ordeal by poison in which guilty persons are exposed by succumbing to draughts of a poisonous

3

substance whilst innocent persons, drinking from the same vessel, suffer no bad effects.

"But it is the cannibals that you are interested in, the gentlemen cannibals I mentioned earlier. The difference between your cannibals of the Ubangi and those of the Ivory Coast is that the latter are recognized officially by the government authorities in much the same manner as the different tribes and religious sects are recognized in this part of the world. They are not considered, nor, in fact, are they criminals like your Ubangi man-eaters. With them, man-eating is a creed—a religion— call it what you like. The French Government is using persuasive measures to suppress the habit but they never think of resorting to force. That is done only when police officers, soldiers or messengers happen to find their way into a stew pot or in the case of the Leopard Men who do not belong to the Gueré cannibal tribe.

"Along the Sassandra River there are several cannibal kings, respected citizens who keep in regular touch with the authorities and pay frequent visits to the various administrative posts. I spent some time with two of these kings and I discussed the subject of cannibalism with them frequently and fully. They both explained that the hunting and eating of human beings is a centuries-old custom with them. A custom that originated way back in history when people were killed in tribal wars and faction fights. The bodies of the dead were then eaten, perhaps in the first place as an act of vengeance, and on finding the meat much superior to any other, it developed into a habit—a necessity. The Gueré did not believe in killing friendly visitors like myself or their neighbours with whom they lived on amicable terms. That was a despicable act, fit only for the criminals and scavengers like the Leopard Men, and such crimes justly merited the punishment meted out by the authorities. I remained in the village of one of these kings for more than a week and was treated with the greatest courtesy and respect. During my stay there I was given a room in the king's 'palace' and had all my meals with him as he considered it would be a discourteous act to allow me to cook my own food whilst I was his guest. This arrangement caused me considerable uneasiness for I am a little fastidious about the kind of meat I eat and for that reason I took the greatest care to examine the daily fare thoroughly without causing my host any offence.

"I found the tribe superior physically and morally, more prosperous and independent, and certainly far more hospitable than the neighbouring Yafouba tribe who are not addicted to cannibalism. They live in larger, cleaner and better ventilated huts than the Yafoubas and are comparatively wealthy in their possessions of goats, sheep, poultry and cattle. The Sassandra River near by provides endless supplies of fish and hippo meat and game is plentiful all over the forest. But in spite of all that they still resorted regularly to man-eating. In their case man-eating is strictly a habit and is not necessitated by hunger as is the case with the cannibals of the Ubangi. It is merely a custom and the meat is much better than any other. Thus, if a man is killed accidentally or in a fight, or dies from a non-contagious disease, the meat is eaten, and if this source of supply does not suffice, they have other means, 'quite legal', to procure the occasional change of diet.

"The meat is prepared in the shape of fries, roasts and stews, and is eaten with rice, vegetables, salt and red-pepper. My host was a native of more than average intelligence and quite a philosopher in his own way. He was willing at all times to discuss the subject with me at length and often replied to my questions by posing his own which I did not always find easy to reply to.

" 'How can you possibly live in harmony and friendship with a man today and put him in the pot tomorrow?' I asked.

" 'How do you white people live amicably with your cattle

and goats one day and kill and eat them the day after?' he
queried.

"I had to agree that such unfortunately was the case, but
reminded him that there was a great difference between a
human being and an animal. The former after all is possessed
of a soul—a conscience—whereas the latter is not similarly
endowed.

" 'Oh, no,' he protested, 'that is not true. You white people
tell yourselves that story so as to justify the killing and eating
of animals. The truth is that every animal, fish, fowl, tree,
stone, river, mountain and plant has a soul—a spirit. When the
body is killed the soul departs and all that is left is meat which
we eat in the same way as you eat animals.'

"I had forgotten that these people implicitly believed that
each and every entity—man or mountain—was possessed of a
soul, a spirit, and that these spirits were responsible for all their
joys as well as their sorrows. It was quite obvious that my host
believed that cannibalism was right and proper as sincerely as
I did that it was not, but my objections to the procedure made
no visible impression on him.

"The day before my departure the king arranged a great
war dance as a farewell gesture to me. It was held early in the
morning in a clearing in the forest about a mile from his village.
I was invited to attend with my entire staff—porters, gun-
bearers and interpreter. The dance was an impressive, savage
display, accompanied by the usual invocations and appeals to
the gods. That night I sat down to a farewell dinner in my
honour for I was due to leave at daybreak the next morning.
I enjoyed a well-prepared meal, and after distributing several
gifts to the king and his entourage I retired for the night.

"Early the next morning I allocated the loads to my porters
and each moved off in turn. But one load was not claimed, the
porter was missing and I told the interpreter to sound his whistle
and call the man.

" 'It will be no use calling for him, sir,' he replied. 'They killed him yesterday morning and you helped to eat him last night.'

"The very idea brought on an attack of nausea and I quickly put my finger down my throat, but that did not help me much. So you see, although it was done unknowingly, I also practised cannibalism, and when I come to think of it, the meat was as good as any I have ever eaten."

After I had listened to Pierre's story and his appreciation as to the quality of human flesh when properly prepared, I thought it advisable to keep a close look-out for the rest of our journey but the trip was completed without undue worry.

4

A DATE WITH DESTINY

Teddy fonton, which is probably a distortion of the name Thornton, was a half-caste; his father was one of the early European farmer settlers in Matabeleland, who married a Matabele woman, and Teddy was the first of their numerous progeny. In spite of his strong European strain, Teddy's mental outlook was almost completely "native".

I first met him when I was busy organizing the final details for a big safari in the month of July. As I stood checking over the stores and provisions for my safari he suddenly appeared on the scene, introduced himself, and expressed the wish to join me on the trip. He stated that he had had a considerable amount of hunting experience and claimed to be "as good a shot as you will find in these parts"—a fact he proceeded to demonstrate on noticing the expression of doubt on my face. He was indeed as good a shot with a rifle as I was likely to find anywhere, whereas with a six-shooter his ability was something quite fantastic and reminded me of the Wild West exhibitions I had so often seen on the screen. In addition to his ability as a shot, he was possessed of a magnificent physique, for he stood well over six feet, weighed over 180 lb., and could not have been much more than twenty-five years of age. I looked upon his advent, and eagerness to join the safari, as a bit of good luck, and a few days later we were on our way to the Kafue Flats in Northern Rhodesia.

The main object of my safari was to collect a couple of good tuskers and as many buffalo hides as possible, for buffalo hides were in strong demand at the time and prices were very good. Also, on my file there was an order from America for two good lion masks—male and female—which I felt certain I would be able to collect on this trip.

Game was plentiful on the plains and Teddy proved a great success in his daily outings. The elephant and buffalo side of the business provided no serious difficulties, but for some unaccountable reason, lions were giving this part of the country a wide berth, and during our first fortnight of hunting we heard them in the distance only on one night. Twice previously I had suggested to Teddy that we should go higher up in the plains to look for lions but he showed a marked lack of interest and was anxious to reassure me that our luck would soon change. When a week later our luck had not changed for the better and an old native hunter informed me that lions were plentiful, and causing trouble at a village named Manwala, I decided to waste no more time and that same night we were on our way to Manwala, where we arrived late the following afternoon. The next morning I went out early and shot two zebras for my camp requirements. The rest of the meat I used later in the day for a "drag" of some three miles in circumference and a goodly portion to tie to a log near a big tree in which I intended to sit that night and wait for any stray lions in the vicinity.

When I was ready to take up my position in the tree that night I invited Teddy to accompany me, but he turned down my invitation saying that he did not feel too well and was not very keen on shooting lions in the dark. My first night in the tree brought no results and on the two following nights I fared no better and, as on the first occasion, Teddy had turned down my invitations to accompany me. I was somewhat puzzled at this, for although the occasion did not arise whilst we were hunting for elephant and buffalo earlier, I had no doubt that he would acquit himself well in a tight corner.

My invitation to him on the fourth night brought a further

refusal but that night my luck changed and, shortly after I had taken up my position for the evening's excitement, a big male lion put in an appearance at the bait and went down to a well-placed brain shot. I was so intent on watching the male that I did not notice a female quite close behind him and she promptly made off after the shot was fired. It did not take long to collect the necessary porters and by nine o'clock that evening we were sitting round the camp-fire discussing the night's doings whilst other natives were busy removing the skin.

Teddy sat listening intently to the discussion when one of my trackers suddenly remarked to him: "If you had not been such a coward and joined the master tonight we could easily have had two lions. The female ran off in a great hurry after the male went down and she will not come back here again for months. You could have helped the master by shooting the female and there was nothing to be afraid of, she would not have climbed to the top of the tree to harm you."

"So you think I am a coward for not going out tonight?" Teddy replied. "Perhaps I am, but if *you* knew that you are condemned to be killed by a lion, will you go out of your way to look for trouble? I am not afraid of any animal in the bush —not even a lion, but since I know that a lion will one day kill me I am not taking unnecessary chances. I have shot as many lions as anyone here tonight, but I stopped hunting them the day I looked at my father's mutilated body. A lion killed him and he could easily have avoided that trouble if he had listened to the Mganga. She warned him on several occasions but he would not listen. The same woman warned me in the same way as she did my father. That was the day we buried him, and from that time onwards I have left the lions severely alone. But before that I had several narrow escapes and I know how easily a man can be killed if he is unlucky. If you are interested I'll tell you about it and you can judge for yourself."

There was an immediate response from several of the natives

near the fire. They were all anxious to hear Teddy's story, and he continued:

"It was that morning when I saddled my horse and went in search of a herd of stray cattle. I took with me a sporting rifle and my two revolvers which I always carry with me for safety. That day I rode for many hours before I came to a large hill which I decided to mount so as to get a better view of the surrounding country. When I arrived at the top of the hill I studied the plain below very carefully with my binoculars. After a while I spotted the herd grazing about two miles away. They were in fairly open country, and as I sat looking at them I suddenly noticed three crouching figures stealthily advancing towards the unsuspecting cattle. I had no difficulty in identifying the stalking figures, they were three lions—a male and two females—and they were just about to enter a thicket of dense bush which would provide good cover for them to approach closer to the herd. I quickly mounted my horse and rode off at great speed towards the thicket.

"When I approached within five hundred yards of the spot where I had last seen the lions, I dismounted and walked cautiously in their direction. Farther ahead the cattle were still grazing peacefully, and some hundred yards to the right was a young bull who had strayed from the herd. He, also, was grazing peacefully, quite unaware of the danger that threatened.

"Up to this point I had seen no more of the lions, but I knew that they were taking cover in the thicket and that they would attack as soon as they thought conditions were right. I was afraid to enter the cluster of bush for fear I would walk into serious trouble, and whilst I stood thinking what would be the best thing for me to do there was loud snorting and great confusion as the cattle suddenly stampeded and rushed in my direction. They had scented the lion who had gone above wind to drive them in the direction of the waiting females, which is the lion's way of hunting.

"The young bull was the last to become aware of the danger, and he was rushing madly to try and join up with the herd when one of the lionesses suddenly leaped from cover and landed on his shoulders. He was brought down in an instant and bellowed loudly while the lioness growled savagely as she tore at his throat. I was barely a hundred yards from them and I quickly trained my sights on to the lioness. After I had squeezed the trigger she made a great leap into the air and fell down back on the struggling bull. She was growling and snarling louder than ever whilst the bull kept on grunting and groaning. I again took careful aim and this time the lioness rolled over dead.

The herd of cattle was by now many hundred yards from me and the other lioness was close behind them. I fired three shots at her but could not tell whether I had hit her or not. However, she quickly abandoned the chase and entered a cluster of bush. For the moment I did not worry about her or the cattle but walked towards the lioness I had killed. As I had emptied my magazine, and not expecting further trouble, I slung the rifle over my shoulder. I had walked only a few paces when I heard a rustle in the grass in front of me; a second later the head of a huge male lion appeared above the grass, less than five paces from me. He looked at me with a terrible scowl on his face and immediately started to bare his fangs and drew his ears back. That was a terrible moment for me, but I luckily managed to pull both revolvers from my belt and, before he could start his charge, I was shooting at top speed with both guns. I was in such a panic I just kept on shooting—not troubling to see whether I was hitting or missing, but when I heard a click, click, as I kept on squeezing the triggers, I suddenly came to my senses.

"The lion was lying flat on the ground with his head on his front paws, and only one of his hind legs was moving as he kicked out helplessly. I knew that he was dead, but before I went closer I reloaded my guns and, taking careful aim, I put two more shots into his brain. When I examined the carcass I found that four shots had crashed into his head and five others into his chest and sides. Even at that short range I had missed five shots, but that must have been due to nervousness for normally I can shoot a mouse at a much greater distance. That was not the only narrow escape I had with lions, and it did not worry me too much after it was all over for I did not know then that my next encounter with a lion would end in such a terrible tragedy.

"That happened on the day when I accompanied my father in order to round up our cattle in the plains. We left home on horseback early in the morning. My father had with him a heavy calibre rifle whilst I took a light sporting rifle and my two revolvers. After the cattle had been rounded up and left in the charge of the herd boys, we decided to go in search of big game. It was late in the afternoon when we saw a big herd of wildebeeste in the open plain. As they were grazing out in the direction of close forest, it was decided that I should circle round the herd, cut them off from the dense bush, and drive them back to where my father would wait for them under cover of a big tree. In this way the animals would find themselves between two fires, and with careful manœuvring we should account for several before they could scatter and get beyond shooting range.

"With this object in view I rode round the herd and started to drive them to where my father was waiting. Everything was working out well and in about five minutes the herd should have been close enough for my father to start shooting. Now, suddenly, while the animals were still beyond his range, a shot rang out; this was followed almost immediately by another. Shortly after that I could hear the savage growls of a lion and in the distance I could see a riderless horse running at top speed. It was obvious to me that there had been an accident and I immediately spurred my horse and rode at top speed towards the spot from where the growls came. A few moments later I pulled up, a hundred yards from the terrifying sight of a big male lion standing over my father and tearing away at his flesh. I moved closer and from a distance of about twenty yards I could hear my father calling faintly for help.

"This was a terrible situation for me to be in, for the lion was crouched so closely over my father than even a well-placed shot would have been extremely dangerous. At the same time, I realized that the longer the lion was left undisturbed the sooner my father would die. Up to now the lion had shown no sign that he was aware of my approach. I decided to move up still closer, and by shouting loudly I hoped to attract his attention and that he would then move in my direction and give me a chance to place a shot. When I came within ten yards I quickly dismounted, raised my rifle and took careful aim and then shouted on the top of my voice. The lion immediately came to an erect position and stood scowling at me with his head well raised. It was still a dangerous situation but I decided to take a chance.

"As I squeezed the trigger I saw the lion slump down on the prostrate figure of my father. In this position a second shot was impossible so I stood for a few moments and watched the lion closely. At the end of quite two minutes he still showed no signs of life and Father also was lying motionless. I pulled both revolvers from my belt and walked up cautiously to investigate. The shot I had fired at the lion had entered the brain and he was quite dead. A close look at my father convinced me that he, too, was dead. It was a distressing thing to see and I quickly tried to pull the lion from my father's body, but I was trembling so much and felt so weak with the shock that I was unable to move the big beast. I walked back to my horse, took a long piece of rope which I always carried with me; this I tied to the lion's hind leg and attached the other end to the saddle and spurred the horse to drag the lion from my father's body. There was nothing else for me to do but lift his body on to the horse and tie it to the saddle and return home.

"It was after the funeral that day when Mganga warned me that a similar fate awaited me. You will understand now why I try to avoid having any trouble with lions. The Mganga is never wrong."

Teddy's explanation made a visible impression on his listeners for, like all other natives, they were firm believers in the clairvoyant abilities of the witch-doctor, and knowing this, I did not blame Teddy for keeping in the background when I set out in search of my two trophies. We remained in the Mamwala camp for another week, but as no other lion ever came near the bait I decided to return home where the safari was disbanded a week earlier.

It was quite three months later when one of my old hunting boys came up to me and said: "You remember that young fellow Teddy who accompanied us on the last safari?"

"I remember him quite well," I replied. "Is there anything wrong with him?"

"Oh yes, *bwana*, there is plenty wrong with him. A lion killed him two days ago. He followed a wounded buck into long grass and there he found a lion busy eating it. If he had left the lion alone and walked away slowly all might have been well, but he started shooting with those two little guns of his and he must have hurt the lion badly for it left the buck and attacked Teddy immediately. The boy who accompanied him managed to escape into a tree and watched it all. Teddy never had a chance after the lion jumped on him, but it is true that the lion died a little while after he had killed Teddy. Those little guns of his were much too small for a big lion. . . ."

My mind went back to the night when Teddy had asked: "What would *you* do if you knew that you were condemned to be killed by a lion?"

Teddy probably would have avoided all trouble if he had left the lion on its prey, but the ever-present fear of being killed by a lion must have prompted him to try and kill the beast before it could attack him. On the other hand, it is possible that he was not the victim of faulty judgement but that he was merely keeping a date with destiny.

5

THE ADDICT

I was sitting in an hotel in Mombasa waiting for a boat which would bring a friend from America whom I had arranged to take out on an extensive safari in Kenya and Tanganyika. On my arrival at the hotel I found a telegram awaiting me to say that the boat was being delayed at Beira and would be at least two days late.

Mombasa offers very little in the way of distraction for one who had spent most of his life in Central and East Africa, and for the want of something better to do I decided to bring my diaries and notes up to date during my enforced stay.

It was as I sat on the veranda of the hotel, checking over some scripts that a tall, dark, well-dressed stranger came over to my table.

"Do you happen to be a brother in affliction?" he queried. "My name is Harold X, I am a free-lance journalist and do a good deal of work for a well-known news agency in South Africa. Seeing you writing and checking over scripts made me think that you are following a similar profession. I hope I am right?"

I invited him to be seated and explained that although I was not actually a journalist, I was nevertheless busy preparing material for publication. During further conversation he told me that he had arrived from Aden only a few days earlier and had not quite decided whether to visit Kenya before he returned to Johannesburg where he lived. He became quite interested when I told him the reason for my presence in Mombasa and the proposed safari. By the time we prepared for bed that night we had discussed many topics and Harold was showing an even greater interest in my forthcoming trip.

The following night he again joined me at my table and after some casual talk he asked: "What are the prospects for me to join you on your hunting trip? I am not particularly interested in hunting as such, but a few weeks away from everything may do me a lot of good. If it is necessary, I will procure a gun and I'll be only too willing to contribute my share of the expenses."

I explained that I was not professionally engaged for the trip but that it was a friendly arrangement with my American friend who I had not met personally but with whom I had been corresponding for some years. So far as I was concerned, I had no objection to his joining us, nor did I think my friend would object.

The boat docked early the next morning and during the day I introduced Harold to Ellis, my American friend. The matter of Harold joining our safari was quickly settled and two days later we left by train for Nairobi, from where the safari was to start.

There was a very marked difference in both character and the appearance of my two companions. Ellis was a stocky, well-built man with a happy-go-lucky nature. He was suffering from a severe dose of "huntitis" and lived every moment of the trip. A hunt in Africa was an ambition he had nurtured ever since early childhood, and his happiness now was complete. Harold, on the other hand, showed only a passing interest in the hunting side of the business and seemed more in his element when we gathered round the camp-fire at night and discussed current topics under the warming influence of a bottle of Scotch. Although he could not be described as a morose individual, it soon became obvious that there was something weighing heavily on his mind. On occasions I had watched him sit in deep meditation and talk to himself.

I was not exactly surprised when, at the end of ten days, while sitting round the camp-fire one night, Harold looked at me and said: "I do not wish to appear ungrateful, but I'm afraid the bush has not provided me with what I came to seek. If it could be conveniently arranged I would like to get back home as soon as possible."

Ellis, who thought that the safari so far had surpassed his highest expectations, was quite unable to understand Harold's attitude and immediately started to emphasize the many advantages to be gained by continuing the safari—the fascination of bush life, the adventure and excitement of the hunt, and last, but not least, the pleasant evenings round the camp-fire where one could discuss the events of the day in pleasant surroundings and in a wonderful climate.

"You are quite right, my friend," replied Harold. "It is easy to see that you are very happy and that you have found what you are seeking—adventure and excitement. I, on the contrary, came here to escape from a life and conditions that brought me too many painful memories. I thought the bush would be the ideal place to bring forgetfulness, but I find that it isn't so and for that reason I would rather return."

In the bush, more than anywhere else, one avoids asking personal questions, and so far as I was concerned no further explanations were necessary. But Ellis, a typical example of American warm-heartedness, became profuse in expressing his sympathy and insisted that there must be some way of helping Harold to forget—if only we knew what it was that our friend wanted to forget.

For a while Harold sat staring at the fire, then, shaking himself as though he had just awakened from a dream, he continued: "Maybe I will feel better if I told someone my story. This is perhaps as good a time and place as any, but it is a long story and I may weary you with it. As soon as you are tired of listening you must tell me."

4

Ellis was quick with an assurance that such a thing was not remotely possible and that we would listen to the story for the rest of the night, if need be, and Harold proceeded:

"It was at an hotel in a charming inland town in South Africa where I first saw Isadora—a most vibrant and glamorous personality. Dining one night, my gaze aimlessly wandered round the room when I noticed this lovely woman. Her black wavy hair was loosely coiled in the nape of her neck and her dark eyes gleamed as she talked animatedly. I fell to speculating what her nationality was, her appearance indicated Spanish origin—probably from South America, for her toilet suggested it. She wore an excessive amount of jewellery—bracelets and elaborate ear-rings. Every time I glanced in her direction I met her eyes. She was with a male companion and I dared not return her smiles.

"Dinner finished, I retired to the lounge for coffee and a cigar. Soon afterwards Isadora came in too. I noticed the slenderness of her figure, but she carried herself gracefully. She was still chatting and laughing, but before I realized what had happened her companion was asking me if I would care to join them for liqueurs. I accepted, and the night that followed was one of the strangest in my experience. I had no sooner sat down when she set about ridding herself of her companion. For this I could hardly blame her for he appeared rather stupid and was completely dominated by Isadora's personality. In fact he behaved something like a lap-dog. I noticed with some amusement that when she did not wish to discuss anything or answer a question she simply dismissed it with a flutter of her hands or a shrug of her expressive shoulders.

"It transpired that she was French, born in Algiers, and she immediately addressed me as 'chéri'. We chatted gaily and it was after ten o'clock when I succumbed to her invitation to bring my bathing suit and drive her to the sea—some twenty miles away. The road was rather trying at night owing to the

numerous winding sharp bends and no one but Isadora could
have persuaded me to take that drive at that hour of the night.

" 'I'm longing for a bathe,' she said, 'and the night is young'
—a remark I was to hear many, many times in the days to
come.

"She snuggled closely to me as I drove and the wonderful
night with the beautiful woman beside me heated my blood
like wine. Arriving at the deserted beach, we changed into our
suits; she wore a tight fitting white satin suit which gave her
slender figure a wraith-like appearance. We ran hand in hand
into the breakers like two carefree children, and for an hour we
revelled like sea nymphs with only the moon and the frothing
breakers for company. It was with some difficulty that I finally
persuaded Isadora to get dressed and return home, for she loved
the sands and the sea. When we left the beach the moon was
already dipping towards the horizon.

" 'I do hate going to bed, *chéri*,' she protested. 'We never
know whether we will ever wake again.' The underlying reason
for this remark I did not fully realize at the time.

"For several days before our meeting I had been working
very late at night and this night's unusual events helped to add
to my fatigue. Isadora, on the contrary, showed not the slightest
sign of fatigue, and her every movement was gay and expressive
of youth and the joys of living.

"The next day I looked for Isadora at lunch, but she had not
come down. I was soon to learn that she never appeared until
dinner and that it was rare for her to retire until the small hours
of the morning.

"Life soon became extremely strenuous for me. I had creative
work to do during the day whilst Isadora slept, and my nights
were spent in her company. I had, of course, fallen in love with
this strange exotic creature whom I did not understand. I tried
hard to persuade her to change her mode of living, only to be
told that the night was the time for love and romance. My

nocturnal existence became very full, for I had to think of, and plan all manner of things to amuse Isadora. This was not always easy in the restricted life of a small town. But theatres and long drives helped to fill part of the night programme and then there were the many nights on the beach where we laughed and loved and forgot the cares of the day. But often now the dawn found me weary and I had difficulty in keeping awake on the drive back home. Isadora, on the contrary, was always as gay and fresh as when we started.

"It was not very long after this that I began to notice a haunting expression of fear in her eyes. I begged her again to let me help her lead a more normal life. For a moment she looked worried and then replied: 'No, no, you do not understand. I am happy this way, I have always been accustomed to it. If you love me you will try to understand.'

"I did try to understand, but I felt worried, for her appearance deteriorated slowly, she began to look ill and was intensely nervous—so much so that in time I became suspicious and wondered whether there were other men in her life. Her mode of living was quite beyond my comprehension and it was not possible for me to check up on her movements between dawn when I left her and at night when I saw her again—sometime after dinner, for I was occasionally kept busy at my desk. It happened sometimes that I called at her apartment during the day, only to be told by her maid that she was not to be disturbed and that no food was taken to her whilst she slept. I realized then why she was so thin—emaciated in fact.

"The strain of this strange nocturnal life was telling heavily on me and I thought of a bold solution: I would marry her, and in this way I would be able to alter her mode of living. I made up my mind to put the proposition to her at our very next meeting. But that meeting was unexpectedly delayed for I did not see or hear from Isadora for three full days. I phoned her room but there was no reply and I began to picture all manner of things. I was about to open her door forcibly when her maid informed me with the greatest earnestness that madame was not to be disturbed under any circumstances whatsoever. She herself had been instructed not to enter the room until she was called for. She assured me, however, that madame was not ill and that there was no need for me to worry. It was several months later that I discovered that the maid was well paid for her services and loyalty.

"When at last Isadora did appear I was perturbed to see the dark shadows under her eyes and the hot burning look in their depths. I tried hard to get her to talk about herself but all she would say was: 'Please, *chéri*, it is nothing. I am very well. If I wish to lead my own life and to sleep for three days it should not disturb anyone—I often do that.'

" 'Well, I agree, you must sleep sometimes, but you do not eat and you are looking very ill. See how thin you are!'

" 'Not at all,' she replied, 'of course I eat, and I have always been thin.' With a shrug of her shoulders she ended the conversation.

"We again resumed the old life. But my days were weary and lonely without her, and when I kissed her good-bye each morning I did not know when I would see her again—a day, two days, three days, perhaps never.

"To my proposal of marriage she would only reply: 'Not yet, Harold, not yet.'

"Five more months passed in this manner. I adored Isadora, but I understood her no better than I did that first night I met her. It was at this time that a very rich gold strike in the Free State attracted my attention, and as a journalist, I thought it would be good for me to visit the place. I decided to go there for a few weeks. I sensed that Isadora was relieved when I told her about my intentions for she hurriedly promised to write to me regularly during my absence—a promise she failed to keep. I kept myself busy on the job as I was anxious to get back to Isadora. Three weeks later I was back at the hotel and immediately went to her apartment. I felt puzzled when the maid told me that 'Madame has gone out.' For Isadora to be out at 11 a.m. was something very unusual, but I did not question the maid and sauntered into the bar lounge to refresh myself with a cold beer.

"I had not been there many minutes when Isadora left the hotel in the company of a strange-looking man. He was slight and tall, wore a cream-linen suit—perfectly tailored—and a fez. A long Egyptian cigarette holder dangled between his thick lips. It is, of course, a very usual and normal thing in the East, but in South Africa it is extremely rare to see a white woman walking in the company of an Oriental. I instantly drew back as they passed. They were engaged in earnest conversation and I gained the impression that he was giving her orders. I was not only unhappy, but greatly intrigued by this turn of events. Later that afternoon I unobtrusively turned over the pages of the visitors' book and there I found his name. He was obviously an Egyptian and his last address was an hotel in Aden. It was all very mystifying, and when I asked the receptionist about Isadora, she replied: 'Oh, she will be back next week.'

"When Isadora returned the following week she was extremely nervous and her friend of the fez had disappeared. I expected her to tell me about her strange companion for she did not know that I had seen them leaving the hotel. But she never mentioned him and later that night she remarked casually: 'I have been to town (meaning the beach where we had gone so often), Harold, I had some shopping to do for I am going away soon.'

" 'Where are you going?' I asked, trying hard to hide my anger.

" 'I cannot tell you that, but I will write.'

" 'The same as you did before?' I was furious and taxed her about her friend with the fez.

She accused me of having watched her but grew calmer when I explained that I had seen her leaving the hotel on the morning of my return. She went on to say that, being born in Algiers, it was natural for her to be cosmopolitan in her outlook and that it was quite normal for people of different races to mix freely. I beseeched her to tell me where she was going but she became agitated and asked me not to insist. She begged me to trust her and promised again to write and explain everything to me in good time. She came up to me and kissed me, tears running down her cheeks. I had a presentiment then that I was saying good-bye to her for ever.

"The next day she packed hurriedly and I saw her off at the station. After she was gone I became forlorn and depressed. I drank too much and could not concentrate on my work. The thought of Isadora and her association with the man of the fez tormented my mind until I decided finally that I would search for her. But where? As I stood talking to the receptionist one afternoon, I suddenly hit on an idea. The visitors' book. She must have given her previous address when she signed the register. I was friendly with the receptionist and in a casual manner I turned our conversation to the subject of Isadora. 'She is a lovely woman,' offered the girl, 'and she lives in Aden —how romantic!' 'Did she leave a forwarding address?' I queried. Isadora had left no forwarding address, but whilst I stood talking I aimlessly turned over the pages of the visitors' book until at last I found what I was looking for. Her previous address in Aden was the Hotel Geneva.

"I waited for news from Isadora, but somehow I knew it would never come, so I decided to put my work in order and if, at the end of a month there was still no news from her, I would go to Aden, find her, and bring her back as my wife. I kept extremely busy for that month and anxiously awaited news which never came. On the first of the month I called at the steamship company and got a reservation for the 15th, and

on that date I left Durban on the s.s. *Angola*. As she steamed
out towards the East I felt happy for the first time in weeks.
The heat along the coast was intense and I spent most nights
walking the decks and wondering what kind of reception
awaited me should I find Isadora in Aden. We docked at night
and the gaudy little bazaars were all open and ready for the
tourists—offering black coffee and scented cigarettes for added
attraction. I immediately proceeded to the hotel Geneva and
booked accommodation, after which I sauntered out to find my
bearings. The hotel is only a few hundred yards from the little
square which is the centre of attraction in Aden. Here one finds
the vendors of jewellery, silks and perfumes, the beggars and
guides. I was soon strolling down the narrow alleys and ended
up at a café where a tired-looking girl was dancing barefooted
to the monotonous Arabic music. Later that night I returned
to the hotel and started making discreet inquiries. Isadora was
not known there, but her friend of the fez was a permanent
resident. He was the owner of one of the largest bazaars in
town. This much accomplished, I turned in for the night and
slept until daylight, and after a hurried breakfast I went on my
mission.

"I crossed the sun-baked square with its hundreds of loiterers
and soon found myself in a street of bazaars; at the far end was
the one I was looking for, the largest and most sumptuous of
the lot. A few steps down a staircase I entered a large room,
dimly lit by lamps with rose silk shades. The air was musty
with heavy odours of incense and Eastern perfumes. There were
numerous brass tables on which were displayed a vast collection
of silks, dressing-gowns and ornaments. A large show-case contained an amazing selection of jewels—diamonds, rubies and
semi-precious stones in a variety of settings. The counters were
littered with bottles of perfume of different sizes and shapes.
As I stood looking at the show-case the man with the fez suddenly appeared.

" 'Excuse me, M'sieur,' he said, 'I did not see you enter; of what service can I be?'

"I was taken aback for the moment but quickly came to the point.

" 'I am searching for Isadora and I think you are in a position to help me find her.'

"I detected a startled look in his face but he did not lose his poise as he answered: 'I'm afraid I cannot help you,' and started to move off.

"But I was determined not to be put off in this manner and continued: 'I saw you in the hotel M. with her in South Africa and I have traced you back here from the address you left in the visitors' book. Isadora is here in Aden and you must know where she is.'

"For a moment he appeared to be in deep thought and then invited me to be seated. 'You are quite a detective, M'sieur. Tell me, why do you wish to find Isadora so urgently? You know, of course, that she is not known here by that name? I know where she is, but that is of no value to you for I am not at liberty to tell you.'

"I formed an instinctive dislike of the man, but decided that my purpose would be best suited if I humoured him and told him everything.

"He listened to me attentively until I had finished and in an expressionless tone he remarked: 'Very well, I see that you are determined to find her so I will help you, but before we go further I advise you to prepare yourself for an unpleasant shock,' and saying this he beckoned me to follow him.

"We walked down a narrow passage and came to a large elaborately draped room in which there were a dozen or more cubicles all draped with heavy silk curtains of Eastern design, and the lights were very dim. Suddenly my guide stopped before a cubicle at the far end, and pulling aside the curtain he pointed to a sleeping figure on a divan. I stooped down, and to my horror I found myself looking upon the pale, death-like features of Isadora. I called out her name twice but she did not move.

" 'No, it is no use, my friend,' said the man beside me. 'She will remain like that for many hours yet.'

"I stood there completely dazed as he slowly drew the curtains together, and in a stupor I followed him. In the front room again he invited me to be seated and offered me a cigarette which I accepted mechanically. I was speechless, for the shock had completely unnerved me.

" 'She is drugged?' I finally muttered. 'What is Isadora doing in this place?'

"He looked at me for a moment or two and then in a voice which carried a suspicion of pity he replied: 'This, M'sieur, is a den of iniquity. The *élite* of Aden come here to satisfy their craving for morphine, hashish, opium and other amusements according to their taste.'

" 'But Isadora,' I interrupted him, 'what is she doing here?'

" 'Yes, I'm coming to that, M'sieur, you must be patient, it is a long story and not a very pleasant one.'

"He prolonged my agony by lighting another cigarette and slowly fixing it in his holder. At last he leaned back and looked at me.

" 'Isadora,' he said, 'was one of my best agents. She worked from Algiers to Cairo at first and later on a much wider circuit. She was concerned for a long time with energy-giving drugs—cocaine, benzedrine, caffein and so forth. Then came the time when she began to suffer from insomnia,' he shrugged his shoulders and knocked the ash from his cigarette, 'so, morphine was the solution. She is dying, soon it will all be over.'

"The look on my face must have softened him a little, for he added: 'I'm sorry, it is all very unfortunate, but I will look after her till then. I would advise you, M'sieur, to go away and forget what you have seen here. Aden is a strange place and people who know too much have been known to disappear mysteriously.'

"He rose and escorted me to the door politely. I staggered from that place. I wanted to walk, to think, to be alone. I wanted to rid my nostrils of the musty smell, the stifling air, the heavy drapings that shut out all light. Poor Isadora! I could not get the vision of her lying there out of my mind for an instant.

"The week that followed whilst I waited for my ship was indeed sad for me. I went to the bazaar on several occasions, but Isadora was always sleeping and I could not speak to her. 'Does she not eat?' I asked an attendant. 'No, not much now. She sometimes sips tea. The end is very near now.'

"I understood so much of the past now. Those nights on the beach, the nervous energy, her hot, burning eyes, the days of sleep—it was all so clear now. On my last day in that tropical port I called at the bazaar again, hoping that I might be able to see and talk to Isadora once again for the last time. The doors were closed but I kept on knocking until they finally opened silently. The man with the fez stood facing me.

" 'Aren't you opening today?' I asked him.

" 'No, M'sieur, not today. We have a funeral to attend to.'

"I stood staring at him and he slowly nodded his head. Then he silently closed the door.

"That, my friends, is my story. I hope I have not bored you," Harold concluded.

Although it was past two o'clock in the morning, Harold's story certainly did not bore us. After he had finished we all sat in silence for several minutes. I felt lost for words as there was obviously little to say. It was one of those situations where opinions or advice are not of much practical use. Ellis probably was thinking on similar lines. His considered opinion, however, carried a lot of logic in it. "Your trouble, Harold," he said, "is not geographical; it is mental. The best way to live it down is to try and find something that will take your mind away from it all. There is nothing like hard work and concentration to help you in this case. Go back to your home—not to sit and brood on what has happened, but try and find consolation in hard work, and don't forget, there is always as good a fish in the sea as ever came out of it."

Harold remained with us until we reached a native village a week later and there we engaged the necessary porters to take him back. Five years later I had occasion to visit Johannesburg and took advantage of the opportunity to call on him. He was happy to meet me again and invited me to spend an evening with him at home. There he introduced me to his charming wife and baby son. We did not refer to the story he told us round the camp-fire that night, but it was quite obvious that he was very happily settled.

A month later, on my way to Europe via the East Coast, our boat docked at Aden for two days. I did the rounds of shops and bazaars, and as I stood looking at a large show-case in which there was a most elaborate display of jewels and perfumes I wondered if the owner was a tall Egyptian with a fez.

6

IN DEAD MAN'S COUNTRY

I WAS CAMPED at a spot way down on the Zambezi River when one of my scouts came in one afternoon to report the arrival, a few miles away, of a game ranger who had just returned from "Dead Man's Country".

Dead Man's Country referred to the wild, desolate territory of the Balovale tribe in the Zambezi swamps which is rarely, if ever, visited by Europeans, and I was naturally anxious to meet this European who had braved a safari in this inhospitable and forbidding country. The next day I moved my camp to where the new-comer had settled and found that the man who had successfully completed a six-hundred-mile safari through what must be considered one of the most difficult stretches of country along the Zambezi, was the game ranger, Mr. Kenneth Shannon. That night we sat round the camp-fire and, as may be expected, the conversation soon turned to the subject of the safari my newly-made acquaintance had just completed. Shannon was an excellent raconteur and a full account of his adventures on this trip would be quite beyond the scope of this chapter in which I have recorded only part of his narrative:

"When I left headquarters in a Land-Rover that morning to return to my office at the boma, some five hundred miles away, I had every reason to feel worried, for it had been decided that I would do a safari through the Balovale and Kobombo regions, starting from the Zambezi River. The first three hundred miles of this safari was to be completed by Land-Rover and trailer into which I would pack all my food and trail equipment as well as five orderlies. From the boma at Balovale, where I would receive more detailed instructions from the District Commissioner, I would have to walk south along the Zambezi River as far as the Leper Mission, and from there I would follow an eastern route for six hundred miles through the jungle country of Kobombo.

"My main concern at the moment was the fact that, for the greater part of the journey I would have to depend on the Kabalovale tribe for porters. The Kabalovale is a degenerate, savage tribe, 'eaters of dogs', with filed teeth and cannibalistic tendencies upon whom little reliance can be placed. Further cause for worry was the fact that we were in the midst of the rainy season. This meant torrential downpours and the dangers of crossing crocodile-infested streams—veritable death-traps— and the discomfort of having to hack one's way through the tangled undergrowth at this time of the year.

"It was only a few weeks earlier that my fellow game ranger, Ted, had lost his life in an attempt to save his friend, Johnny, from a crocodile in the Lunga River. Chief Ingwe's men managed, after three days of river sitting, to retrieve an arm and a leg of the game ranger. Added to all this was the fact that I would have to do a certain amount of tsetse research on the way in badly infested country. And last, but not least, my safety depended to a large extent on a heavy calibre rifle, the rear sight of which I had recently re-soldered after it had been knocked off when the rifle had fallen off the bouncing truck on a bad road. It was a crude job that inspired very little confidence.

"The first three hundred miles from my station at the boma to Balovale were accomplished by Land-Rover and presented only minor difficulties, and on my arrival there I reported to the District Commissioner. We immediately went into the details of my forthcoming safari and it appeared that, apart from the numerous routine duties, there were several items that needed urgent attention. The first was a case of man-eating lions which had been reported recently—a story to which we did not attach too much importance. The second was a case of a rampaging hippopotamus which had terrorized a village. The conduct of this animal, we felt certain, was due to the fact that it had been wounded by natives using muzzle-loader rifles. I had recently had the unpleasant duty to destroy a hippo which had fallen victim to these inferior weapons. This unfortunate creature was in a pitiful state for it was unable to enter the water as it was suffering from numerous festering sores which became targets for the fish in the pool. Being prevented from entering water must have caused the animal as much agony as did its open gaping wounds.

"The third item on the list was a more difficult proposition. News had been received from a village on the outskirts of the elephant country that three native hunters had set out on an elephant hunt and were six weeks overdue. For several days the villagers had gone in search of them but without success. As a rule, when native hunters go out in a party and run into trouble, there is generally one or more survivors to come back and tell the story. In the present case the men had simply vanished and left no trace. We decided that this case needed immediate investigation.

"After my programme had been decided I began to feel uneasy and restless. The unfortunate deaths of my two friends still weighed heavily on me, and since the last accident I had frequently awakened at night in a cold sweat dreaming about crocodiles in heavily infested pools—the kind of pools I would soon be crossing on my trip. I consider myself a good swimmer, but so were Johnny and Teddy, but that did not save them from the saurians. On my present journey I would have to cross numerous swamps where crocs often lie in the long grass to sun themselves. The only way to negotiate the rivers was by native canoes, most of which had an unpleasant way of capsizing in stretches of water where the crocs were most numerous.

"Early the next morning a body of twenty porters gathered outside the boma office. I explained to them the objects of our safari, pointing out the dangers and hardships to be encountered, but I assured them that I would look after them to the best of my ability. I fully expected that some of them who might be acquainted with the difficult country we were about to enter would refuse to accompany me. It turned out, however, that none of them knew anything about that part of the country and an hour later we were marching along the banks of the Zambezi River, my scouts and heavily laden porters strung out in a long line behind me.

"That first day was very hard going as my objective was a Mission station twenty-five miles away. It was essential for us to make that point as it was the first place along our route where the necessary foodstuffs for my native staff were obtainable and, rather than go hungry that night, the porters agreed to do the extra ten miles.

"At the Mission I procured sufficient maize meal, etc., to last for ten days. We then left for the Kabompo River, which we reached five days later. The Kabompo River was the first of many really bad spots on our journey, for it runs through a heavily infested tsetse belt. Apart from the risk of contracting sleeping sickness, we had to contend with the painful stings of these flies. A tsetse sting gives one the impression that a red-hot needle is entering the body. There is no effective method of escaping from these pests other than travelling at top speed in order to pass through the belt in the quickest time possible, or otherwise to make a detour so as to avoid contact. In my case, I had to go through the belt so as to collect specimens for future study. After I had obtained the necessary specimens we crossed the river and settled at a spot on the opposite bank which was free of tsetse. Here we spent a day to enable me to replenish meat supplies.

"That afternoon, accompanied by Gibson, my gun-bearer,

and six porters, we set out in search of game. Gibson and I were walking ahead of the porters on a game path. When I looked back to see if all was well with the porters I was amazed to see an enormous buffalo bull walking some five yards behind the last porter. I quickly shouted out a warning on the top of my voice and called for Gibson to hand me the heavy calibre gun. When those porters looked back and saw the bull within a few yards from them there was a mad scramble for the surrounding tree-tops. The bull, on the other hand, came to a sudden stop and appeared to be even more surprised than the natives. The startled look on his face seemed to indicate that he was cursing himself for being fool enough to walk in a dream in the belief that he was following the rest of the herd. Before I could get in a shot he disappeared in the long grass.

"After all the excitement had died down we started to trail the bull. We had not gone very far when Gibson came to a sudden stop and pointed ahead of him. This time it was not a buffalo, but an enormous eland bull with his dewlap almost touching the ground. He was quite unaware of our presence and, aiming carefully for the heart, I pressed the trigger of my 7 mm. rifle. The bull stumbled to his knees and then miraculously recovered from the shock and set off at a fast pace. My shooting was at its very worst that day for it took six more shots to bring him down. He was a fine specimen and I estimated his weight to exceed 2,000 lb. I distributed as much of the meat as possible to each carrier for the first load and then returned to camp.

"We had not walked far when Gibson swerved from the path and shouted: '*Nyoka, bwana.*' I did the natural thing and that was to look on the ground in front of me. But it transpired that the danger was overhead, for in the branches of a small tree a fourteen-foot python lay coiled up waiting for his next victim—a role which, for the moment, I appeared to be destined to fill. The snake was lying quite motionless and I had no difficulty in shooting it. To satisfy myself of the assertion that a python's heart will beat for a full day after it is killed, I removed the heart and held it in my hands for quite half an hour. It was still beating away merrily, but at that stage I lost interest and threw it away. For all I knew, it kept on beating for the rest of that day.

"The shooting of the eland delayed us for a day to enable the natives to smoke and dry the meat. We then pushed on to the last village to be found on our way to 'Dead Man's Country'. On our arrival there I decided to stay over for two days in order to procure more foodstuffs for my staff. Two of the orderlies were sent ahead to the Kamwedzi River to scour the country for the missing hunters. At the present village I had serious trouble with my porters who had now decided that they had had enough and wanted to return home. In the end I won them over with threats and generous supplies of meat which I managed to shoot nearby.

"On arriving at the Kamwedzi River there was no sign of the two orderlies and this worried me considerably that night. But early the next morning they put in an appearance and brought good news. During the two days in which they had scouted the forest they had come across three large elephant herds and had seen several bulls with outsize tusks. Only two hours earlier they had seen an enormous tusker accompanied by a young bull. On picking up the human scent, the big bull had immediately started to trumpet, and the scouts were hard put to escape from his wrath. Of the missing natives, however, they had found no traces. For the rest of that day we were occupied in erecting suitable shelters against the heavy rain. That night the camp reverberated with animal noises—lion, leopard, hyena and jackal—they were all there in force to make the night hideous.

"Early the next morning we were on our way to search for the missing men. A few hours later we came across an open clearing in the centre of which stood four well-preserved huts. A fifth had recently been pushed over—obviously by an elephant. In a square between the huts lay the scattered remains of a hartebeest, not more than two or three days old. The doors of the huts were all open and there were lion pug marks all round. Inside the huts I found fresh ashes scattered in all directions and near the extinct fires there were the usual calabashes and cooking pots. It was quite obvious that the huts had been vacated in a great hurry. In addition to the lion spoors there were numerous elephant tracks. It was easy to see that the huts were raided, first by a lion, and then by an elephant, for the latter's spoors were the fresher of the two. All the indications went to show that disaster had overtaken the last occupants and that from now on we might have to look for their remains—at the same time keeping a sharp look-out for the lion and the rogue elephant. This was an assignment I did not like very much in view of the defective sights of my heavy calibre rifle, and less so when I noticed that it was Friday the thirteenth of the month.

"It was late in the afternoon when we caught up with the two elephants. The peculiar malformation of the right front foot of the bull made it clear that he was responsible for pushing down the hut we had seen earlier in the day. He was an enormous brute with a pair of magnificent tusks. The other bull was a much smaller and younger animal. They were quite two hundred yards from us when we first saw them. It was a stifling hot day after the downpour of the previous night and not a breeze could be felt. Even by testing the wind direction with cigarette ashes we were unable to tell in which direction our scent would be carried. The old bull looked a dangerous customer and I did not fancy the idea of starting operations over a range of more than twenty-five or thirty yards so I decided to crawl up cautiously. By the time I had reduced the distance separating us to fifty yards I was sweating profusely and my mouth was completely parched. It was during the next twenty yards of crawling that misfortune overtook me.

"Up to that point the big bull had been grazing in the open and offered a splendid target if I could get within shooting range. Now the younger bull walked up and stood directly in front of the big fellow. Whilst I was busy crawling to the side to get the old rogue lined up in my sights the young bull suddenly stopped feeding and lifted his trunk high. Obviously, he had picked up a whiff of scent. I decided, there and then, to get him out of the way as soon as possible and before he could alert his companion and start a charge. As he stood sniffing the air I aimed for a spot between his eye and the ear and squeezed the trigger. As the bullet struck home all four of his legs buckled under him and with a great crash of breaking branches and saplings, he rolled over on his side, to all intents and purposes quite dead.

"The sudden crack of rifle fire and the collapse of his friend thoroughly alarmed the big bull and he immediately took off at top speed. I went up to the fallen beast and examined the carcass. The bullet had torn into his brain and he died without knowing what had struck him. We then immediately started to follow the other trail which led into extremely difficult country —the kind of country in which an encounter with a rogue elephant would be distinctly dangerous. The going, in consequence, was very slow, and when, by sunset, we had failed to make contact, I decided to camp for the night in an insect- and mosquito-infected swamp.

"Shortly after daybreak the next morning we were once again on the trail, the marshy ground made tracking quite easy, but a low mist hung over the swamp and visibility was exceedingly poor. Quite frequently we were startled out of our wits by antelopes rushing out of the tall grass quite close to us. It was two hours later when one of my trackers came to a stop and beckoned me over. Quite close by we could hear the rumbling of an elephant's stomach. The spot from where the rumbling came was a veritable death-trap, for the grass and reeds there were fully ten feet high and visibility was reduced to about two yards. I waited for ten minutes and then decided to advance slowly, foot by foot, in the direction of the rumbling sound. It was tricky work, for at any moment I expected to see four tons of elephant coming down on me. After I had advanced fifty yards in about as many minutes I could see the top of a red ant-hill a few yards ahead of me and I decided to make my way cautiously to it. The stomach rumbling had now ceased and all round me there was an oppressive silence of death.

"With two orderlies behind me, we finally reached the ant-hill, and on stealthily peering round its side we spotted the bull looking intently at a spot some distance to the side of us. He was standing at the edge of the long grass, his ears flapping backwards and forwards and his trunk slowly swaying from side to side. It was quite obvious that he had scented danger and was on the alert. He showed all the signs of being a real nasty customer and all he needed was to determine our exact where-abouts before he would come out in full charge. Under the existing conditions and from a distance of about fifty yards, it was much too dangerous to attempt another stalk—even now time was running out rapidly. At that distance, with an un-reliable rifle, a heart shot would be too risky so I trained my sights for his brain and waited for him to stop moving his head. A moment later I pressed the trigger and I knew instinctively that I had bungled the shot and missed the vital spot. He immediately swung his huge head in the opposite direction, spread his ears out wide and, raising his trunk aloft, he gave vent to the most unearthly screams. Those blood-curdling screams of blind rage were enough to turn one's blood into water. And now, at the most critical moment, an astonishing misfortune befell me.

"As I rapidly drew back the bolt to ram home another slug,

the two remaining bullets in the magazine catapulted over my shoulder. This is a peculiar defect in that type of rifle which is used extensively by game departments, on which several reports had previously been made. Luckily for me, I did not lose my head in this critical situation but quickly took another shell from my shirt pocket and rammed it home. All this was done in the matter of a second or two. By this time the bull had worked himself into a mad frenzy. His trunk was swinging rapidly from side to side in an effort to pick up our scent and his huge body was swaying as he stood stamping his feet into the ground. All this while he kept up those blood-curdling screams. There was no time to lose for it was obvious that the very next moment would bring things to a head.

"It was as I raised my rifle for the next shot that the bull took off in full charge. But I could see at once that it was a blind charge and that he had failed to pick up our scent, for what little wind there was sat in our favour. He was rushing in a straight line a little to our left and I immediately realized the danger that, on passing us, he would pick up our scent and wheel back on us. All I could think of at that moment was that I wanted like hell to get as far away from that spot as possible and in the quickest possible time, but it would have been suicidal to start running at that stage and I kept him carefully in my sights. The moment he came in line with us, barely twenty yards away to the side, I aimed for the heart and pressed the trigger; there was a violent jerk of the huge frame and, to my relief, the bull seemed to accelerate his pace in a straight line. As he went on his way we could hear him crashing through the forest for some distance and then all was silent. That was the moment for us to vacate the scene in a hurry.

"We ran at top speed to an open clearing about fifty yards away and then stood listening intently. There was not a sound to be heard anywhere. That meant that the bull was either dead or he was picking his way carefully through the dense forest. We waited for several minutes and then started walking in a wide circle round the cluster of dense bush where the bull had disappeared. Three hundred yards farther we came to a heavy blood trail which we followed for quite a mile in fairly open country and then we saw the bull again. He was standing near a large Mutondo tree with his ears flapping slowly and his head well down. It was quite obvious that he was mortally wounded. I stalked up within twenty yards from the rear and aimed carefully for the base of his spine, but as I was about to press the trigger he turned round and offered a perfect target for a brain shot. A moment later a heavy .404 bullet ploughed through his brain and he rolled over on his side. I walked up to the huge carcass and, just to make doubly sure, I fired another shot into his brain.

"For a long while I stood looking at the great carcass, but strangely, there was no feeling of elation. Somehow, I felt sorry about the whole business, for even the enormous tusks brought me neither profit nor satisfaction as they were to go to the Game Department as government trophies. During the many years I served with the Game Department I had thousands of encounters with elephants, but this was the first occasion on which I was forced to shoot any of them. The lion? We never saw a sign of him, and in spite of a prolonged search, we found no traces of the three missing men. Their disappearance will remain for ever one of the mysteries of the bush."

7

TWICE LUCKY

WHEN THE FAMOUS *prima donna* Clara Butt toured South Africa many years ago, she brought with her a first-class orchestra. The first violinist of that orchestra was Ernest, a dark, slender, good-looking young man of about twenty-five years of age. When the company reached Johannesburg most of its members mixed freely with the local population which, unfortunately, included a good sprinkling of unsavoury characters—a not unusual thing in the history of all gold rushes.

It was not very long before Ernest found himself on terms of close friendship with a couple of particularly unsavoury characters, and the upshot of this friendship was that the trio raided one of the city's banks on a Saturday night and departed with a large sum of money. When the robbery was discovered on the following Monday morning, the culprits were a long way from the scene of the crime, and once safely beyond the immediate reach of the police, they divided the spoils in equal proportions and parted company.

Ernest's two companions were arrested in due course and sentenced to long terms of imprisonment but he himself managed to elude the police net, and before long he landed in what was then known as German East Africa, and even if the South African police knew of his whereabouts, there was very little they could do about it, for at the time there was no extradition agreement between the two countries.

Elsewhere I have written at length about Ernest's escapades in East and Central Africa and related the story of our meeting at Kasama, from where we travelled together for part of the journey to Kashitu in Northern Rhodesia. At the time of our meeting Ernest was recovering from the after effects of an unfortunate encounter with a wounded buffalo, and it was whilst he was laid up with a pair of broken ribs and a fractured leg that he contracted a dose of black-water fever which very nearly carried him off.

Ernest was extremely lucky to escape with his life in his last encounter with the wounded bull and this was due entirely to the timely intervention of his gun-bearer at a moment when the bull had him on the ground and completely at his mercy. The story he told me one night as we sat round the camp-fire on our way to Kashitu was about yet another amazing escape from a wounded bull, and made his previous escapade look quite tame by comparison, for in all my years of experience in hunting buffaloes I never heard of a case where the victim of an attack managed to administer the *coup de grâce* whilst he was seated on the back of a badly wounded bull and effected an escape with only superficial injuries. The incident is very well vouched for, as it was confirmed by the gun-bearer in question, and Ernest himself, whatever his other faults, was certainly not addicted to the telling of tall stories where his own personal exploits in the bush were concerned—on the contrary, his failing was that he often erred on the side of modesty and restraint. I can do no better than give the story in his own words as he related it to me that night:

"It is a strange thing that, of the many scores of buffaloes I have shot over the years, I have had only two tussles with wounded bulls, and in both cases my escape was nothing short of miraculous. Perhaps this was due to my good luck in earlier hunting and to the fact that I never indulged in 'snap-shooting' where buffaloes were concerned. I always used the heaviest possible calibre against them and never fired a shot at any of them unless I felt quite certain of an outright kill—even now, in my present condition, I can still call my shots on any range up to three hundred yards. The fact that I hunted buffaloes without trouble for so long was undoubtedly responsible for my later carelessness in which, on two occasions, I came within inches of losing my life.

"On the morning of this last incident I had trouble with my old gun-bearer after he had been out on a night's spree and was still suffering from the after effects of over-indulgence when I was ready to leave shortly after daybreak. I decided to appoint Kasembe to the job for the day. Kasembe was a raw native who had had years of experience in the bush and was a first-class tracker, but his hunting experience was confined to the use of the bow and arrow and on occasions the old muzzle-loaders which many natives in those parts employ. He had never used a modern rifle and knew nothing of its mechanism, for during the time he was with me he was never allowed to handle any of the rifles.

"When we left camp on the Muhezie River that morning I handed him my .375 rifle and took particular care to see that the safety catch was on 'safe' so as to avoid any possible accident that might result from careless handling when crawling through dense bush. I myself carried the heavy .425 calibre elephant gun as I expected to find buffaloes close to a water-hole in the river. At the pool we picked up the tracks of a herd which had come to drink during the night, and in little more than an hour we caught up with them in close forest country.

"I had plenty of time to examine the animals carefully for they had taken up their position under a big tree in a clearing, and at a range of two hundred and fifty yards they were quite unaware of our presence. I finally selected an enormous bull who had, what I considered, the largest spread of horns I had ever seen on a buffalo. I took particular care about this shot and trained my sights on the heart. When I saw the spasmodic jerk which generally follows a heart shot, I had no doubt that, in spite of his burst of speed as he took off, he would not run very far before he would drop down dead. I had seen the same thing happen before on dozens of occasions after well-placed heart shots.

"When we got to the spot where the bull had 'taken it' and followed his tracks, we found a heavy blood trail which indicated clearly that the shot was well placed in the heart or in the lungs. I decided that it would be advisable to leave the bull alone for a while and went near a big tree in the shade of which I got the natives to make a fire, and I prepared tea and had a leisurely breakfast of tinned meat and bread. We remained under the tree for quite an hour, at the end of which time I felt certain that the bull would be ready for dissecting. As we walked on the blood trail I noticed that the splashes of blood became larger and heavier as the bull went along and this made me feel even more certain that he was dead by now. As a result, I did not keep as careful a look-out as I would have done normally—in spite of Kasembe's warning to be careful.

"My eyes were still fixed on the blood trail which led to a cluster of bush when there was a vicious snort only a few paces ahead of me. Before I could raise my rifle or realize what was happening, I found myself flying through space. The bull had hooked one of his horns in the belt of my bush tunic and the resulting toss had landed me several yards from him. My rifle had been knocked from my hand at the moment of contact. With no means of defending myself I decided that my best plan would be to lie down as flat as possible—a position in which the bull would not be able to lift me so easily with his long curved horns, and hoping as I did, that Kasembe would soon be on the spot and go into action with the rifle he was carrying.

"After the bull had tossed me and I had landed—almost cat-like on all fours, he stood looking at me menacingly for a second or two and, having decided that he had not finished the job properly, he came straight for me. There was not much time for proper observation but I could see that the bull was in a very bad way and hard put to keep a straight line as he tottered towards me. Of Kasembe, my last hope of salvation, there was not a sign to be seen anywhere. In the next instant the big brute was standing over me and tried desperately to lift me again. There was none of the snap that usually attends such an attempt and I immediately grabbed his horn and hung on for life, and then came the vicious swing of the head as the bull tried to toss me again. My legs went whirling through space, but I hung on grimly to the horn. As my body swung over it felt as if both arms were being pulled from their sockets, but now I found myself, half lying, half sitting, on the bull's neck. I at once clamped my legs round his neck in a vice-like grip and hung on, ape fashion, for all I was worth, all the while shouting for Kasembe on the top of my voice. The bull was trying frantically to dislodge me whilst he was tottering slowly towards a tree where, I had no doubt, he intended to crush me to death against the heavy trunk. But before he reached the tree he once again came to a stop. It was obvious to me that he was so weak from the loss of blood that it was difficult for him to keep erect, and the vicious swinging of his head had not much force behind it.

"It was whilst I was in this desperate position that Kasembe at last put in an appearance a few yards away. I shouted frantically at him to shoot as quickly as possible, but the fool stood there with rifle raised unable to fire a shot.

" 'The trigger has become stuck,' he shouted at me.

"At that moment I cursed myself heartily for having taken such great care to secure the safety catch that morning. I shouted at Kasembe to move the safety catch over, but that was quite beyond his comprehension. By this time my arms were beginning to feel so numb from the strain of hanging on that I feared the next swing of the head would land me on the ground several yards away.

"I was still hanging on grimly and trying to think of some way to escape from my terrible predicament when I felt a sharp dig in my ribs. Kasembe had crawled up from the back, unnoticed by the bull, and was now trying to hand me the rifle. But at that moment there was yet another vicious swing of the head which all but sent me flying through space a second time. That effort seemed to fatigue the bull greatly, for there was a violent shudder of the great frame as he started to lower his head slowly. Kasembe was once again busy pushing the rifle into my ribs. That last violent shake of the head had taken the last little bit of resistance out of my arms and I knew I would not survive the bull's next attempt. I never prayed so earnestly in my life as I did at that moment for the bull to remain stationary whilst I release my grip with one hand to grab the rifle from Kasembe. I signalled him with my head to move forward a little farther and then, in a do or die effort, I grabbed the rifle, at the same time tightening the grip with my knees. It was as the big brute started to lift his head for the next violent shake that I pushed the muzzle of the rifle behind his ear and squeezed the trigger and watched him sag slowly down.

"I have no means of telling how long I sat on the bull's neck clinging to his horns. At one moment my arms were so tired I felt as though I had been there for several hours, but the whole business could not have lasted much more than ten minutes. Kasembe's certainly was a very courageous act and he helped to save my life without any doubt. But more than anything else, I owe my escape to that hour we spent over breakfast. During all that time the bull was losing blood rapidly, for the lung wound must have weakened him tremendously; with only a tenth of his normal strength he would have had no difficulty at all in dislodging me, in fact, it is extremely doubtful if I would ever have landed on his neck at all if he had not been so weak. Those few moments whilst I kept hanging on to the bull's horns for life are amongst the worst I ever spent in my life."

Ernest's claim that he could "call his shots" was no empty boast. In East and Central Africa, where he was a very well known character, he was considered a most deadly shot. The pity of it all is that he did not confine his shooting to animals—even though there may be something to be said in favour of his contention that "most of the vermin on earth walk on two legs". But all that belongs to another chapter in his stormy past.

It was on his arrival in Southern Rhodesia that the long arm of the law caught up with him. He faced trial on a number of charges and got off very lightly. After he had paid his debt to society he went to America, where he married an enormously wealthy widow and settled down on a prosperous fruit farm in California. The good luck that attended him in some of his mad escapades in the bush, however, did not hold good in more peaceful surroundings, for he died in a matter of eighteen months after his marriage.

8

CHIWETA TELLS HIS STORY

CHIWETA IS the only man I have ever met who survived a mauling from both a lion and a buffalo and lived long enough to tell the story many years after the two hectic experiences. I met him on the Lualaba River in the Belgian Congo near a place named Ankoro where he frequently visited my camp. At the time of our meeting, Chiweta had lost all interest in dangerous hunting. I was, as usual, on the trail of buffalo and anxious to enlist him as a member of my hunting staff in view of his intimate knowledge of the country. Chiweta, however, was determined to have no more to do with buffaloes but was always prepared to offer advice and recommend the best areas to look for them. Around the camp-fires at night he soon became a regular and appreciated visitor in view of the many stories he had to tell about his hunting days and his many narrow escapes. The two stories I was most anxious to hear him tell were for some reason scrupulously omitted from his nightly repertoire. These were the two encounters with lion and buffalo which left him with the most hideous scars on face and body I ever saw on any man.

Sitting round the camp-fire one night, I taxed him with this omission and insisted that he should tell us all about it. "You have one half of your face missing and there is that enormous scar in your leg, from your knee to your hip, both were due to hunting accidents yet you never mention a word about them," I remarked to him.

"It is quite true, *bwana*, I do not like to talk about these misfortunes for I hate to think about them. Whenever I think about them I have bad dreams at night and for that reason I would rather forget about it."

Chiweta's reluctance to discuss what was obviously an unpleasant subject to him, was broken down with a couple of strong tots of brandy and a good filling of tobacco, and after some more casual talk, he began: "We'll talk about the lion first, for it was with the lion that I had the first accident which very nearly cost me my life. It was a big mistake in the first place to go out and look for him in such bad country, for he had never killed a man but gave us trouble only when he came to raid our livestock, and we could have got him easily if we had been a little patient and set traps for him instead of going after him. But Mapunde was very angry that morning when he went to his cattle kraal and found that the lion had killed a young heifer that was heavy in calf, and he insisted that we should form a party and look for the marauder. I was the only one who had a gun, but the rest of the party had bows with poisoned arrows and also long assegais.

"We followed the spoor for a long way until it entered dense grass. We then decided to split up in parties of two, and Mapunde and I remained together. We had just got through a cluster of very dense grass when we spotted the lion lying in the shade of a big bush. He was fast asleep after his feed of the previous night and had not heard us approaching through the grass. There was a strong wind blowing towards us and this made the grass rustle loudly so that our footsteps could not be distinguished from the noise of the wind. This gave us plenty of time to aim carefully—Mapunde with his bow and poisoned arrow and I with my old muzzle-loader. When we fired at the lion he made a great leap and ran off into the long grass and I could see Mapunde's arrow sticking in his ribs. I was quite certain that I had also hit him and that he would not live for long as Mapunde's arrow was dressed with fresh poison shortly before we left home that morning. Even if my shot did not do much damage the poison from the arrow in his side would certainly kill him in a very short time.

"We decided to go and sit in the shade of the bush where the lion was lying when we fired at him and wait for half an hour before going on the trail. We had no watch to look at the time, but we sat there for much longer than half an hour before we decided to follow the spoor. We found a heavy trail of blood on the grass, and this, together with the poison from the arrow, made us feel more certain that the lion was dead by now. A little farther on the trail the blood stains suddenly ceased, and in hunting for more signs of blood Mapunde and I became separated.

"I had loaded my gun again and Mapunde had several poisoned arrows in his shield. I was walking with my head bent low, looking for traces of blood on the grass, when there was a terrible roar in my ears right next to me. The shock was so great and the lion so close to me that I never had a chance to raise my gun before the brute sprang on top of me. My gun was knocked from my hands and I had hardly landed on the ground when the lion fastened his jaws on the side of my face. I was shouting on the top of my voice for Mapunde to come and help me and busy trying to pull my knife from its shield when the lion shook me violently and I felt the whole side of my face being pulled away. The lion then grabbed me by the shoulder and started to drag me deeper into the long grass. The pain was so great that everything went black and I lost consciousness.

"I do not know how long it was before I again opened my eyes and found the whole party of hunters sitting around me and pouring water over my face. They told me afterwards that when the lion made that terrible noise as he sprang on me, Mapunde ran away in a panic to call the others to come and help. They came to the spot where the lion had jumped on top of me and followed the spoor for about fifty yards when they

6

saw the big brute lying on top of me without moving. All six of them shot their arrows into him but still he did not move, and when they came up closer to look they found that he was dead. For a while they thought that I was dead too. The poison from the arrow must have overtaken him as he stood over me and he fell down dead on top of me. I was very lucky that none of them hit me with their poisoned arrows.

"But that lion should have died long before he did. I have often seen big antelopes die within a few minutes when they have been hit properly with a poisoned arrow. This lion lived for more than an hour with an arrow sticking in his ribs. If only we had remained under the bush for another half-hour all the trouble could have been avoided. But even so, it might easily have ended fatally for me, for if the poison had not taken effect whilst the lion was standing over me he would certainly have killed me before the others could come to the rescue. The other men carried me to the Mission station that same night, and it was many months before the wounds on my face and body were healed."

Chiweta's assessment of the potency of the poison the natives in these parts use for their arrows was no exaggeration. On this safari I timed an eland cow that had a poisoned arrow shot into her hindquarters. She took off at great speed after receiving the arrow, but within ten minutes we caught up with her. She was then tottering from side to side and a minute or two later she fell down. It was exactly twenty-two minutes after she was hit that she breathed her last. It is, of course, possible that the poison took effect more rapidly in this case owing to the fact that the cow ran at full speed for some distance and thus accelerated the circulation of the poison in her blood.

Yet another demonstration of the deadly nature of the poison, and one which very nearly ended in tragedy, concerned a native marksman who sustained a minor cut in his finger when he pulled at a blade of grass as he was walking along. The cut was hardly noticeable and barely a drop of blood flowed from it. This happened early in the morning. Late that afternoon the native dipped his finger into an earthenware pot containing the poison in order to dress his arrows for the next day's hunt. Within a few minutes he was overcome with violent convulsions and a few minutes later he became quite unconscious.

We were fortunately close to the White Fathers' Mission and the victim was carried there hurriedly. The Fathers attended to him immediately on his arrival and injected serum. The treatment was repeated twice during the night, but by sunrise the following morning the man showed signs of impending death and the Fathers resorted to artificial respiration. A few hours later there were signs of a slight improvement and this continued for three days, when the man was able to walk about again. The Father in charge of the mission told me that the serum was perfected in Belgium and contained a fair amount of strychnine. With their customary generosity, they gave me a good supply—just in case. But the occasion luckily never arose for me to use it.

In view of the deadly action of the poison it is quite understandable why Chiweta took the risk of following the lion in such treacherous country. Just why, in this case, it took such a long time for the poison to act is a little puzzling. A possible explanation is that the arrow was wrapped up in a cloth shortly after it was dressed, and in its fresh liquid state a large amount might have been absorbed by the cloth. It is in this manner that bites from mambas and cobras are rendered less effective if the fangs are driven through the clothing of a victim.

After Chiweta had told the story of his adventure with the lion he sat in deep meditation for a while and then, under the stimulating influence of another good helping of brandy, he continued:

"The buffalo was also a very bad business and I was caught that time because he behaved quite differently to what they usually do when wounded, for normally a bull will try and escape as quickly as possible after he is hit and will not charge unless he is pursued. That morning we also went out in a big party and we had three guns between us. For a long time we saw no fresh tracks and when we came to a big dambo we spread out and walked in a long extended line, for buffaloes often go to sleep in long grass where one may easily miss them by a few yards.

"I was a long way from the man next to me and it was just as I got through the tall grass that I saw the bull standing under a tree—less than a hundred yards from me. He was a very big animal with enormous curved horns and all by himself. I had plenty of time to shoot, for he had not seen me. I aimed carefully for the heart and fired. The moment the bullet hit him he came straight for me. I do not think he intended to charge me in the first place, it was just bad luck that I stood directly in his way, and when he saw me he must have known that it was I who had hurt him and he decided to kill me. It does not take a buffalo long to run a hundred yards, and before I could get out of his way he was ready to hook me. I stepped aside quickly and just managed to avoid the point of his horn, but the outside curve caught me in the side and threw me many yards. The bull was grunting and bellowing loudly, as they always do when they are very angry, and I also shouted at the top of my voice for help.

"I had no sooner landed flat on my face when he came for me again. It was a terrible sight; his eyes were like balls of fire and blood was pouring from his nostrils, whilst he blew froth from his mouth. He came at such a speed that he missed me completely with his horns but he quickly wheeled round to attack again. As he came close to me and was about to lift me on his horn, I grabbed hold of his left front leg and hung on with all my might. If those horns had been shorter he would have been able to hook me very easily, but I could feel the horns scraping on my body as he tried to lift me. It was terribly painful and the grunting was something really awful. All this time the blood was pouring all over my face and body. At last my arms became lame and I could not hold on as tightly as I did in the beginning; that was when he hooked his horn into my flesh—just above my knee—and ripped my leg wide open when he tossed me. When I fell to the ground all the wind was knocked out of me. I was completely helpless, and when I saw the bull coming towards me again I knew that I would be dead in a few moments. I closed my eyes and prayed to the good Lord to help me. It was just then that I heard two shots. The bull made a great dash forward and seemed to forget all about me and ran past me. A few yards farther he collapsed and grunted loudly three times and then kicked out his hind legs. He was quite dead.

"It was very lucky for me that my friends did not run away but came to my help as quickly as possible when they heard the loud grunting and bellowing whilst the bull stood over me as I hung on to his leg. If it were not for the fact that he had such enormous long curved horns he would surely have been able to lift me a second time and kill me long before my friends could come to my rescue. As it is, I nearly lost my leg, and nobody could have looked worse than I did when my friends came to lift me from the ground, for I was covered with blood from head to feet. You see, my shot missed the heart but went deep into his lungs, and every time the bull grunted and snorted in rage whilst I hung on to his leg he sprayed blood all over me. It was terrible, *bwana*, very terrible indeed. Until you have such an experience yourself you will never know just what it is like."

That it was a terrible experience to live through I had not the slightest doubt, for quite apart from the terrible mental strain whilst the action lasted, there was the ghastly scar which ran the full length of his upper leg. With one ear missing and the entire side of his face almost completely bare of flesh or skin, Chiweta's two gruelling experiences with the two great killers had completely destroyed his nerves, and even the memory of it all must have been extremely painful to him. I could quite understand why he felt reluctant to discuss the matter. But even though the subject was distasteful to him, my curiosity prompted me to ask him: "You are the only man I have ever met to survive two such misfortunes, will you tell me now which you consider the more dangerous of these two animals— the lion or the buffalo?"

"Eh, *bwana*," he objected, "that is not the talk of a hunter. If you have two pots—one large and one small, it is easy to tell which will hold the most water. With lions and buffaloes it is not like that; they are both very dangerous animals and unless you are lucky to escape like I did they will both surely kill you easily. But if it is God's will that I should be killed by one of them, I would prefer the buffalo to do it, for when the buffalo kills he does it quickly and he does not frighten one so much as the lion with his terrible roars. Even though a lion is sure to kill you in the end once he has attacked you, it is true that he is a very stupid beast and does not know how to kill a man as quickly as he does other animals."

Chiweta was quite right in his opinion about the lion's lack of *savoir-faire* where human beings are concerned. It frequently happens that a human victim is subjected to a clumsy mauling before he is eventually killed—or escapes. This does not happen in the case of animal victims, for these he kills in very quick time—so quickly, in fact, that it has often been said with ample justification, that the lion is the most humane killer of them all.

After Chiweta had related his two terrifying experiences he asked for another fill of tobacco. I watched him light his old stump of a pipe and draw deeply as he sat looking at the fire in deep meditation. Perhaps he was thinking of some other details of his two terrifying ordeals which he had omitted to

CHIWETA TELLS HIS STORY 87

mention. A few minutes later he rose from the log where he had sat whilst telling his story. "It is late and time for us all to be in bed," he said. "I hope you will have good luck to-morrow and bring back lots of buffalo meat." To which I replied: "I hope you will have no unpleasant dreams this night."

9

RONALD, THE WHITE MAHUMA

One of the strangest characters I ever met around the camp-fire was Ronald. This happened when I was camped on the main road between Hoima and Entebbe, on Lake Victoria, on my return from the Ituri Forest. I was lying on a camp stretcher inside my tent that afternoon after a tiring day when a gang of mashila boys stopped outside the tent door. Inside the Mashila sat Ronald—all seventeen stone of him. He was travel-ling in an opposite direction, for he was bound for the Hoima mission station for medical attention.

His introduction: "Meet Ronald X, the only white Mahuma in Ankole, proud possessor of a prize herd of Ankole cows and High Priest of the Cow Cult," had a touch of the bizarre about it and intrigued me sufficiently to ask for further explanation which was not long in forthcoming.

It appeared that, more than thirty years earlier, Ronald had arrived in Uganda as a member of a Mission society. Some two years after his arrival, as a result of some misunderstanding with his superiors, he had resigned from the society as he felt that their respective views were quite irreconcilable. At that time he had already reached the stage of blood brotherhood with the Bahumas and found the life amongst them more to his liking than the onerous existence of a missionary in those parts. What it all amounted to was that Ronald had "turned native", had become a "milk drinker", and taken to living among the Bahumas and Bunyoro as one of them. During those thirty years he had become an initiate of most—if not all—their strange cults and rites, and he probably knew more about the customs of the different Ankole tribes than any other living European.

In spite of his social lapse, Ronald was a man of great culture and intelligence, and my only regret is that circumstances did not make it possible for us to spend more than four days together, for had that been the case I have no doubt I could have written a complete history of the Ankole tribes from material supplied by this extraordinary character. The present chapter is compiled from notes I made in my diary, and I record them for the greater part in his own language:

"The Bahumas are not negroes in the same sense that we know other negro races in Central Africa, for they originate from Hamitic stock and have kept their race pure as they do not intermarry with other negroes. They are essentially a pastoral tribe and have no interest whatever in agriculture, for their staple diet—in fact, their *only* diet—is cow's milk. It is for this reason that the cow is the most important entity in their lives, so much so, that even time is calculated, not by the sun or the clock, but by the activities surrounding the cows— the time to let them out for grazing, to return them to their enclosures, to milk them, to water them, etc., etc. All these are matters of vital importance to them, for, as I have said, their entire existence depends on the milk of the cow, which they drink all day long. On the rare occasions when they do eat meat it is in order to conform with some sacred rite—usually in connection with the burial of a member of the clan. After they have eaten meat it is forbidden to them to partake of milk for at least twelve hours, for meat, being an impure article, will have a deleterious effect if taken too soon before their sacred beverage.

"This exclusive diet of milk naturally causes obesity (I am, myself, a good example), which is considered a great virtue amongst them, for the fatter the woman, the more beautiful she is considered to be. In order to ensure corpulence, young women are forbidden to do much walking or to take any exercise which may induce slimness. After marriage they grow to huge proportions, so much so that a walk of a hundred yards is quite beyond their powers. Their participation in dances is limited to a seat on a rug, where they sit and sway their arms and bodies, and this they appear to enjoy as much as those taking a more active part.

"Cows supply not only the milk, but also the receptacles in which it is stored, for these are fashioned from the long horns. And the sacred fire which burns continually in every village is fed by cows' dung. This fire, which is never allowed to die, is not used for cooking or heating purposes, but burns night and day in order to keep away evil spirits that may harm the herd.

"Among the Bahumas a man's wealth is estimated by the number of cows he owns, and the animals are held in far greater esteem than their wives, for whereas a sick wife will be treated with complete indifference, a man will sit all day and night to nurse a sick cow, and many suicides have resulted from a cow's death.

"A strange anomaly is the fact that, although a man's wealth is assessed on his possession of cows, they are not really his exclusive property, for all the subjects of the country belong to the king and therefore their possessions are likewise the property of the king. For this reason it is a serious offence to sell a cow to a person of another tribe for such an act would serve to impoverish the king.

"In the matter of morals the Bahumas are probably superior to any other native tribe in Central Africa. A young girl who transgresses against the moral code and commits a breach of chastity is condemned to death by the clan in the presence of her parents, after which she is taken to a river and, with heavy irons tied to her hands and feet, she is thrown into the water and drowned. Here also, the offender is not punished so much because the code of morality has been violated, but because they believe that if an offender is protected the cows will suffer as a consequence. This moral code is applied strictly to unmarried women, but after marriage much greater laxity is permitted and the moral code is often sacrificed in order to comply with the laws of hospitality which, among other things, provide that a guest must be given food and sleeping accommodation. It is not unusual for a guest to share, not only the host's bed, but also his wife.

"As among other native tribes, a dowry is paid to the parents of the future bride. In the case of the Bahumas it is very high and may amount to ten or more cows—a price often beyond the means of the average man. In such cases the difficulty is overcome by three or four brothers, or friends, pooling their resources and the wife then becomes communal property. In most cases the arrangement works out satisfactorily to all concerned. Polygamy is a recognized practice, but only a few can afford to buy more than one wife. Marriages are generally arranged by the parents, and it is not unusual for the couple to see each other for the first time on the day of the wedding. The husband, in addition to the dowry he has paid, will bring a present of a cow or sheep—according to his economic circumstances—and the bride accepts the groom by taking a mouthful of milk and squirting it all over his face. Before the groom can enter the apartment of his wife he has to fight a mock battle with her friends who gather outside her door. These mock battles are not entirely harmless, for often he is badly scratched and bitten and loses a fair amount of blood in the process.

"When a child is born it is taken away from the mother for a week and nursed by an aunt or other female relative, after which it is returned to its mother who nurses it for three years, during which time she lives apart from her husband. At the age

of three months the child—if a boy—is put on the back of a
cow by its father, the cow becomes his property and supplies
his future milk requirements. Girls do not fare so well, they are
the property and care of the mother and bespoken in marriage
before they attain the age of one year.

"The Bahuma is not a savage or criminal tribe. As in every
other community, murder is a most serious crime, but it is not
a crime that is often committed amongst them. The exceptions
are the cases where a person has stolen or harmed a cow. Such
cases are tried by the king or his first minister. If it involves the
welfare of a cow, the accused is generally ordered to pay suitable compensation to the relatives of the murdered man. In
other cases the old Mosaic law of an eye for an eye is applied
and the murderer is sentenced to death. After execution his
body is buried beneath that of his victim.

"In cases of illness or death, appeal is immediately made to
the medicine man who looks for the cause—mostly evil spirits—
and prescribes a cure. If it is an ordinary illness he will give an
infusion of herbs, a localized pain is treated with an iron hot
enough to cause blisters. Illness caused by bad spirits is treated
in the same way as the Bunyoros do, which I will describe later.
When an ordinary person dies the body is buried in the dung
heap of his cattle enclosure on the same day. The grave is dug
to the depth of the dung deposit and may not enter the soil
beneath it. The burial takes place at the time the cows return
from grazing. That night the calves are separated from the
mothers and all night long there is a bellowing and mooing,
which is the way in which the herd expresses its sorrow. The
cows are not milked that night, and neither the calves, nor the
relations of the dead man, are allowed to drink any milk during
the night. The entire family sits in front of the cattle enclosure
and moan and wail until daybreak, when a bull is killed and
the meat distributed amongst the mourners. Mourning con-
tinues until the meat is all eaten. A second bull is then killed

and a branch from a sacred tree is dipped in its blood and hung over the gate of the enclosure. This will prevent evil spirits from visiting the herd. After that the rightful heir to the deceased's property brings over a fresh bull and takes possession. Acting on advice from the medicine man, he may build a new enclosure for the cattle. The death of a woman calls for no special ceremony. She is buried in the dung heap and the husband finds himself another wife.

"Much more serious is illness among the cattle. The chief medicine man is sent for without delay, and being a most important person, a special hut is provided for him during his stay. A bull is killed and a great feast provided. After this the medicine man inspects the herd whilst he listens to the owner who will describe all the symptoms of the disease to him. Another bull is killed and several arteries opened, the flow of blood from each artery is carefully studied, after which follows a minute examination of all the main organs—heart, lungs, kidneys, etc. The medicine man then decides the cause of the trouble. Yet another bull is taken from the enclosure and made to walk round it several times after which it is returned to the herd inside. Early the next morning it is killed, the blood is caught in a receptacle, and all the inhabitants and cattle are sprinkled with it. The body is dragged to the gate of the enclosure, and the inhabitants as well as the cattle jump over it as they leave. In this manner the disease is transferred to the dead bull and, in order to make quite sure, a branch, soaked in the bull's blood, is hung over the gateway so as to prevent the evil spirits from entering the kraal again.

"The king of the Bahumas, which is the ruling class, is not only the supreme ruler of his people, but also the chief priest and supreme judge. The succession to the throne, as well as the details of his daily life, are almost identical to those of the Banjoro tribe which I will describe later. The main differences relate to his death and the rites associated with it.

"It is rare for a Bahuma king to die a natural death. When he is afflicted with a serious illness or attains an age where he feels he is no longer in full possession of all his faculties, he sends for his chief medicine man, explains the position to him, and asks for a dose of poison. The poison is kept in the shell of a crocodile egg and a small quantity will kill in a few minutes. The exact composition of this poison is known to only a few of the most important medicine men. After the king's death his mouth is opened and sacred milk—from the sacred cows of the king's herd—is poured down his throat. The body is then washed with milk, after which it is carefully stitched up in a cow's hide. It is then kept for a day or two, when the village priests will bring a lion cub and announce to the bereaved people that their late king has now taken the form of the lion they see before them. It is for this reason that the lion is considered a sacred beast. If he should happen to kill a man, or any of their cattle, the matter is reported to the medicine man. If he decides that the lion is in fact a reincarnated spirit of a dead king who is annoyed at some act or other committed by one of his people, the medicine man will instruct them to make some elaborate offerings to appease the spirit. If he decides that the lion is an ordinary marauder, trackers are sent out to find the lair of the beast. On finding it they send for the hunters and other villagers to surround the place. Often as many as four hundred men, armed with spears and clubs, will take part in the hunt and destroy the animal.

"Leopards and pythons are also looked upon as sacred creatures. The former harbour the spirits of departed princesses and the latter those of less important people. If they should become a menace to the population the same procedure as in the case of the lion is adopted and they are appeased or destroyed in accordance with the medicine man's instructions. These are the principal laws and habits which govern the lives of my adopted tribe.

"The habits and customs of the Banyoro tribe are very similar in most respects to those of the Bahuma. The main difference is that they are not entirely pastoral people but devote their interests also to agriculture and industry. Salt and iron are amongst their most important industrial activities, and the recovery thereof is attended by many quaint rites, for the spirits control every branch of activity associated with these industries. Salt is recovered from the dry river beds, and at the beginning of the season the king sends a cow or two and a slave woman to the salt spirit. The cow is handed over for safe keeping to the chief priest and the slave woman to his servants. Her firstborn child belongs to the salt spirit and is taken to a sacred pool, where its throat is cut and the blood mixed with the water.

"These priests who represent the different spirits are all wealthy men, for all gifts to appease the spirits are handed over to them for safe keeping. Thus, the iron smelters must make an offering to the spirit of the hills from where the iron ore is taken, otherwise it will not melt properly. The charcoal burners, likewise, must make an offering, otherwise their fire will not heat up sufficiently to melt the ore. At the spot where the ore is to be dug, a goat is killed and eaten by the priests and labourers in order to establish communion between them and the spirits. The blood of the goat is sprinkled on the trees to be cut for the burning of charcoal, and there are special rites to be observed in regard to the selection of the stones which they use for anvils and the hammers and other tools employed in making axes, spears, etc.

"Rainmakers are a greatly respected body and are paid with cattle or goats. If they accept rewards and fail to produce rain they are brought before the king who warns them to produce the goods in a certain time. If they fail to comply they are ordered to sit bare-headed outside the king's enclosure and eat large quantities of meat which has been heavily salted. They remain there, eating and sweating in the broiling sun without water until they produce rain. If too much rain falls they are ordered to produce sunshine. Should they fail to do so the king orders them to sit outside his enclosure and drink rain water until they become ill. It is an exacting profession, but the rain-makers get their own back in a small way by demanding large rewards to stop them from bringing down storms and tempests of wind which would destroy their crops and disorganize the work.

"As in the case of the Bahumas, the Banyoro are also be-trothed in childhood and enter into marriage when the girl is fifteen or sixteen years of age. In ordinary marriages the bride-groom may never again look upon the face of his mother-in-law. If they should both be present at a feast or dance he must sit in a position where he cannot see her, and if they should happen to meet inadvertently he must get out of her way as quickly as possible and divert his eyes from her and hide him-self from her sight. A more sociable feature of a wedding is that the mothers of both parties must attend the wedding feast. Unless they do so the wife may not cook in her new home and they cannot expect children or happiness. If the mothers fail to comply with this rule within a reasonable time the marriage may be dissolved. In no case is marriage ever the outcome of love; it is simply utilitarian and economic, for the daughters of the union can be sold for cattle at a future date and this will enrich the father. In the case of the mother, it is a necessity, for an unmarried, childless woman is despised by the entire com-munity and has no rights in law.

"In all cases wives live apart from their husbands for three years after the birth of a child. This often results in the husband taking a second wife, that is if he has the necessary means. It is, however, quite normal for brothers or friends of the same clan to share a wife so that during a period of separation the hus-band is not condemned to celibacy. Twins are welcomed, and the occasion is celebrated with dances and the beating of drums. Triplets, however, bring serious consequences for the mother, her father and mother, and the three children are taken into the forest and killed. The father is not killed but must be prevented from ever looking at the king again. To ensure this, his eyes are gouged out and he spends the rest of his life in blindness.

"Serious illness is attributable to two kinds of ghosts—local and foreign. In the former case the ghost is propitiated by gifts of goats, sheep or slave women. These are tied to the bed or body of the invalid for long periods so that the ghost can enter their bodies. A foreign ghost is dealt with summarily and harshly, for it is driven out by noxious fumes which may easily kill the patient as well.

"The king must be notified of all deaths in the community and this is quite a tricky business for he is considered to be above all things—even death. To tell him that death has robbed him of a subject is therefore an insult to him. The difficulty is overcome by sending two good runners with a cow before daybreak. They drive the animal to the gate of the king's enclosure from where they shout at the top of their voices that the cow's owner is dead and then take to their heels at top speed. They are chased for a short distance by the guards, who then return and kill the cow and appropriate as much of the meat as possible before sunrise, when the rest is buried. For the sun to shine on the meat of a beast belonging to a dead man will bring bad luck to the entire tribe.

"When a king dies a deep grave is dug in the dung and a hut is built over it. The body is stitched up in a cow's hide and the grave is lined with cow skins. The body is then laid on a bed of bark cloth in the grave. Two of his wives are selected to be buried with him and they take up their positions on either side of him and the grave is filled with bark cloth and the wives are suffocated. Once a year a man from the clan is selected as a reincarnation of the dead king's spirit. He is treated with the greatest respect for seven days, during which time he may make merry with the king's widows who are not allowed to re-marry. At the end of the seven days the man is taken into the forest, where he is strangled, and the body is thrown into the bush without burial services.

"On ascending the throne, the new king sends for all the princesses, that is, the daughters of the wives of his late father, and selects his queen, for he may marry only a half-sister to fill the role of first wife. The marriage ceremony is performed with the usual extravagant rites, after which the new queen takes the oath of fidelity and mounts the throne. After this the king embarks on a wild spree of marriages. First choice goes to the other princesses—his half-sisters—but long before the list is exhausted female scouts all over the country are busy roping in other likely candidates. It is extremely rare for these women to enjoy the king's company for more than one night, and none of them is allowed to give birth to a child in the king's enclosure. Confinement takes place in the home of a selected chief who is held responsible for the child's upbringing. The women are left to enjoy themselves as best they can in the king's enclosure, but they may not have anything to do with other men.

"The rite in which two men enter into blood brothership is an extraordinary ceremony. The two men take up their posi-tions on a rug opposite to each other. Between them an arrow is placed and also the two halves of a coffee berry. First one man takes the arrow and scratches his stomach until it bleeds. A few drops of the blood is caught in the palm of his right hand, into which the one half of the berry is placed. The opposite party repeats the performance and each lifts the blood-soaked berry from the palm of the other with his lips and swallows it. Each man promises the other to be faithful to him and his relatives and friends for the rest of his life. The brotherhood is sealed by a sister or near relative, who shakes them by the hand

Photo : R. M. Kerr, I.R.L.C.S.

A Camp scene in the Rift Valley during the rainy season

Photo : Dr. D. L. Gunn, I.R.L.C.S.

We had arrived at our present Camp the previous day after considerable difficulty

Photo : Coronet Studios

The Sassanga River near by provides endless supplies of fresh fish

Photo : Kenneth Shannon

Somehow I felt sorry about the whole business

Photo : Kenneth Shannon

He was a fine specimen and I estimated his weight to exceed 2,000 lb.

Photo : *Dr. P. D. Swanepoel*

He had never killed a man, but gave us trouble when he raided our livestock

I sat down and aimed carefully between his ear and eye

(*Above*) Harry was trading ivory—mostly illicit —from the natives

(*Left*) The tusks were even better than I expected, and the two together weighed a little under 300 lb.

Photo : Dr. P. D. Swanepoel

The female of the species is more dangerous than the male

Leo in an impressive mood

and blesses them. This ceremony is of particular interest to me, for I performed it myself on many occasions in order to enter into blood brothership with the tribe. Without it I would not have been allowed to enter their most inner secret councils as I have done for so many years—not only as an accepted member of the tribe, but as a priest of many of their cults and adviser in the many problems of their daily lives."

There was a great deal more to Ronald's story which I have not recorded here. At our last camp-fire meeting I could not refrain from asking him how it was possible for a man of his culture and enlightenment to become, not only a member of such a backward tribe, but also to practise their barbarous rites.

For reply he fell back on Shakespeare: "There is nothing either good or bad, but thinking makes it so."

Ronald had obviously found happiness and contentment in his present mode of living and who was I, after all, to question his right or wisdom in selecting this manner of life?

Early the next morning we bade each other farewell and resumed our respective journeys. Several of the natives of my safari belonged to that part of the country and in conversation with them I gathered the idea that, next to the king, Ronald was indeed the most important person in Ankole at that time, and he was highly respected by all the natives who knew him.

It was with great surprise—and regret—that I learned of Ronald's death when I arrived at Entebbe three weeks later, and even greater was my surprise when I was told that he was over eighty years of age at the time, for I had estimated his age to be in the mid sixties. I have often wondered whether the final burial rites in the dung heap of his cattle kraal were extended to him or whether that other brotherhood which he had forsaken so many years before had closed their eyes to the past and given him a Christian burial.

In the Uganda of today there is not room for another Ronald, but many of the strange rites and customs still prevail. These fortunately do not include the barbarous killings and punishments related in his story.

10

THE LION AGAIN

Because "distance lends enchantment" I allowed my old
friend Micky Norton to persuade me to join him in a safari
over the Nyasaland border into Portuguese East Africa and try
our luck in the Gorongoza region of the Sofalo district. Here,
rumour had it, elephants were very numerous and comparatively easy to hunt. The safari to P.E.A. in the end proved anything but profitable, for although elephants were in fact plentiful, we saw none with tusks of more than 50 lb. Apart from
elephants, the country was well stocked with game of all species,
and lions were particularly numerous—and wily. It was a
nightly occurrence for big prides to roar and grunt loudly all
round our camp until the early hours of the morning and then
disappear mysteriously from the scene. During the six weeks
we spent in these parts I only got a fleeting glimpse of one on
two occasions. This, to a large extent, was due to the dense
bush country and the numerous hideouts in the dry river beds
which were almost unapproachable owing to the high grass
and reeds. If our safari brought us little in the way of compensation in so far as ivory was concerned, it was quite rich in other
adventure.

It was whilst we were camped at a place named Tambara
that we met Fernand Montalo—a strapping six-footer who
weighed well over 200 lb. He was an official in the Game Department of Mozambique. Fernand and his safari landed at
our camp late one afternoon; he was then on his way to
Maquire where man-eating lions had accounted for four natives

in less than a month, and curbing the activities of troublesome lions was part of Fernand's duty. During the many years he had served in the game department he had had many exciting adventures with lions and he had an endless fund of stories to tell about these encounters.

Unlike most hunters who had had trouble with the King of Beasts, Fernand held the lion in particular contempt. I never had an opportunity of seeing him in action in the field, but it was quite obvious from the stories he told that luck had played a very important part in most of his narrow escapes. Fernand, however, was not prepared to attribute these escapes to luck, but to the fact that the lion was a very much over-estimated adversary. The soundness of his arguments may be called into question but they are nevertheless worth recording—and more so in view of the fact that his next encounter with a lion was to prove his last and he was buried two days later.

"The indifference to danger which an angry lion often displays in recklessly exposing himself to attack is due to stupidity more than to courage," he told us as we sat beside the camp-fire that night. "In his natural state in the bush he daily sees large antelopes do all in their power to escape from him and he cannot understand why man, much smaller, yet a much greater killer than himself, does not do likewise. It is true that once a lion is wounded and on the defensive he is one of the most deadly dangerous animals to deal with. But even so, his danger is very much over-estimated by many on account of his ferocious appearance and his frightening growls and roars before he attacks. And strangely enough, it is just those precious moments he loses by staging this exhibition that decreases his actual danger, for I have shot many of them while they were busy making a demonstration of fury. In the bush a split second often makes all the difference and the lion has not the brains to understand that.

"I believe that most lion accidents are due to nervousness

caused by the lion's fearful appearance and the nerve-shattering noises he makes at such times. That is the time when one has to keep calm and avoid taking snap shots at all costs. I have proved that not every demonstrating lion necessarily charges, but if he should be further infuriated by a badly placed shot there is nothing that will prevent him from attacking. In my own case, I have always tried to reduce the shooting range to about thirty yards, thereby eliminating the chances of missing the vital spots. It is true that, if a lion is badly wounded at such short distance and charges, it does not leave one much time for a second shot, but even that is not as dangerous as following a wounded beast from long distances, for it is rare for an animal to attack if he has been shot from a long distance; the first thing they do is to try and escape further injury and look for a safe place to hide. If one walks on to a lion or any other wounded animal under such circumstances the chances of escaping a severe mauling or death are very small indeed, and it has been proved that most of the fatal hunting accidents have happened in this way.

"Only last week I had an exciting adventure with a pride of five lions. I had been stalking them for several hours when I spotted them walking slowly in single file towards a cluster of dense bush. The wind was against them and I made a hurried detour so as to be closer to them when they were about to enter the thick bush. I managed to reduce the distance to about thirty yards and sat waiting for them. There were four females and one male, he was walking behind the others. The females had already entered the patch of bush, but just before he reached this point the male stopped and looked in my direction. I had him well covered and sent a bullet through his heart. He made a tremendous leap in the air and fell down dead. It was just as I got to my feet to walk up to the carcass that a female emerged from cover. Immediately she saw me she drew back her ears, crouched low, and started growling viciously. Whilst she was busy staging this frightening exhibition I carefully lined her up in my sights and placed a bullet between her eyes and she fell down dead beside the male.

"It was another case of losing valuable time before attacking, for had she made a rush for me the moment she saw me I do not think I would have been able to place my shot before she was on top of me, for a distance of thirty yards requires only two big leaps by an unwounded lion. If the lion will take a leaf out of the buffalo's book and not waste so much time in useless demonstrations he will rate as the most dangerous of all animals in the bush. I have never seen a buffalo bull making any kind of demonstration before he goes to work. So you see, the very display of frightfulness which adds to the lion's reputation of danger is actually responsible for his undoing when he faces an experienced hunter."

On the face of it Fernand's views carried a lot of logic and his technique in hunting lions appeared to be as near fool-proof as possible. But in the hunting of dangerous animals no plan is ever completely reliable or safe, and this was proved again in the case of Fernand, for when he went out to settle the score with the man-eater at Maquire things worked out according to expectation for only part of the way. When he got on to the trail of the lion, which happened to be in bad country, he reduced the distance to a minimum before shooting. But in spite of the short range, his shot was badly placed. This time, however, he did not have to deal with a lion who wasted time in making frightful demonstrations, and before he could place a second shot the wounded beast was on top of him. The native gun-bearer who accompanied him lost no time in looking for safety in a nearby tree, from where he sat and watched the subsequent tragedy of which he later gave a graphic description:

"When the lion attacked the *bwana* stood up to him and grabbed him by the throat. The lion was making a terrible noise and blood was pouring from his mouth. The *bwana* was a very strong man and he managed to keep the lion's jaws from his throat. But during the struggle I could see the lion's hind claws tearing at his leg. After a while they both fell to the ground, but the lion did not attack again. He stood looking at the *bwana* for a while and then walked away. When he had walked about twenty paces he went down and lay growling loudly whilst a lot of blood came from his mouth.

"The *bwana* was very weak by this time and could hardly move, but he managed to turn over on his face. His gun was lying next to him and he picked it up. Close to him was an old withered tree trunk, and on this he leaned his rifle and took careful aim and fired. The lion's head fell on its front paws and I knew that he was dead. I quickly ran over to see if I could help the *bwana* but there was nothing that I could do. The blood was streaming like a river from one of the deep cuts in his leg and a little later he stopped breathing. Apart from the deep gashes in his leg there were no other serious wounds."

The gun-bearer went on to explain that the attack came so suddenly that there was nothing he could do to help his master. In order to climb the tree in a hurry it was necessary for him to discard the rifle he was carrying, but even if he had retained it he would not have been able to use it during the struggle without endangering his master's life. A medical examination subsequently proved that Fernand died from loss of blood and that there were no other injuries serious enough to have caused his death.

During the rest of our stay in this part of the country I had the unpleasant experience of being charged by an old rhino bull one morning. Rhinos were particularly numerous here and, unlike in other parts of Central Africa, the natives were not particularly afraid of them, explaining as they did, that they were not aggressive towards human beings as they were not molested by hunters because of the game restrictions. In view

of my previous experience with *bicornis* and his unsavoury reputation in the matter of charging without provocation, I should
not have placed any credence in this story. Rhinos, more than
most other animals, form very regular habits. Thus, if un-
molested, they will drink regularly at the same pool for long
periods, and after their early morning feed they will go to rest
—often standing out in the broiling sun whilst they sleep. I had
no licence, nor was I interested in rhino hunting, and apart
from keeping a sharp look-out ahead of me and testing the
wind direction frequently when we came across fresh tracks, I
did not worry much about them.

That morning there was a strong wind blowing across the
plain in which there were numerous clusters of dense bush.
There were no fresh tracks to indicate the presence of rhino in
the vicinity, and as there was no game in sight I was walking
somewhat aimlessly by myself some fifty yards behind the
trackers with my rifle slung over my shoulder when there was
loud snorting in the cluster of bush some thirty yards to my
right. The next instant an old rhino bull came out at full
charge, blowing off steam as loudly as any steam engine I ever
heard. As the natives who walked ahead of me had passed that
point only a few seconds earlier without incident, I had no
reason whatever to suspect trouble and certainly could not have
fired a shot in time to stop the charge. Luckily there was a small
tree quite close to me and for this I made a wild dash at top
speed. I was still busy making my way up the small trunk when
the old bull rushed past still blowing steam at full blast. For
quite fifty yards he ran at top speed, then came to a sudden
stop, turned round and stood sniffing the air for a while and
walked off in the opposite direction, apparently quite satisfied
that all danger had passed.

The natives were greatly amused at the incident and forthwith explained that it was the white man's smell that had upset
the old brute. That may, or may not, be the case. The fact is

that, with better eyesight and less impetuosity he could have made life very uncomfortable for me that morning. The little tree I had climbed certainly would not have resisted the shock of a full head-on charge had he rushed into it. However, I was afforded an excellent opportunity to watch carefully and make a mental note of what an ill-tempered rhino bull looks like in full charge. With horn lowered, tail on end, the loud snorting and blowing and something like three tons to back him up, it would be distinctly unhealthy for one to stand in the direct line of his charge. We remained in this area for another week, during which I had yet another narrow escape from a buffalo which I had wounded, and then we moved off to the Barue country where we saw one of the most barbaric demonstrations of native witchcraft which I will describe in the next chapter.

I I

THE ORDEAL BY POISON

During my wanderings in the African bush I have come across many practical demonstrations of native witchcraft in its most primitive and barbarous forms. This is a profession that thrives on ignorance, credulity, and the superstitious fears of the masses of illiterate people. Whereas I am prepared to admit that I have seen witch-doctors perform strange feats for which I could find no ready explanation, I am convinced that the average "Mganga" is a charlatan of the first order—the extent of whose nefarious work is limited only by the restraining hand of the law—that is in places where observation and control are possible. In the back blocks where the law is administered by village headmen and chiefs of districts, the Mganga operates with complete freedom, for as often as not, the headmen and chiefs are, themselves, under the domination of the witch-doctor and will rarely take the risk of exposing these frauds to the proper authorities. I am further convinced that no native, irrespective of the educational standards he may attain, is ever entirely free of the belief in witchcraft.

When we camped at a little village near Gouveia in the Sofalo district of Mozambique that afternoon, there was an abundance of meat available for the entire population, for earlier in the day we had shot a hippo bull and also an enormous buffalo, quite close to our camp. This ensured meat for those members of the population who, on religious grounds, were forbidden to eat hippo meat. The camp-fire that night presented a scene of animation, for it was only on very rare occasions that these natives could gorge themselves to their hearts' content on freshly killed meat. But in spite of their keen anticipation of the great feast which awaited them, a current of subdued restraint could be detected amongst the villagers as they sat in small groups discussing amongst themselves.

None of the members of our safari could speak the local dialect, but there were several men from the village who spoke Swahili quite fluently and when, later in the evening, the village headman, accompanied by a Swahili interpreter, came and joined us at the fireside, the conversation soon veered to local affairs. He had not been with us for long when he explained that the lack of gaiety and dancing was due to the fact that a very serious function was due to be performed the following afternoon and this had somewhat dampened the ardour of his people. He told us that the chief sorcerer of the district had arrived at the village and would investigate the case of one of the villagers who claimed that both his wife and daughter were the victims of witchcraft. The wife had recently died and the daughter was lying critically ill at that moment. The bereaved man was not able to put his finger on the person who was responsible for these misfortunes and for that reason he had appealed to the Mganga to identify the culprit. The investigation was due to take place at four o'clock the following afternoon and if we cared to witness the proceedings we would be welcome to attend.

He went on to explain that this was one of those complex cases that could not be settled by himself, and the witch-doctor, in his superior knowledge, would find the culprit by applying the recognized method in such cases—the ordeal by poison. The entire population would assemble at the appointed place and time and the Mganga, guided by a spirit, would carefully scrutinize each person until he "found" the culprit, who would then be given an opportunity to contest the accusation by swallowing a draft of Muabvi bark prepared by the witch-doctor. If the accusation was false the victim would establish his innocence by vomiting the concoction. If he was in fact guilty, the poison would kill him without doubt, which was the right and proper punishment for a person who is guilty of unauthorized witchcraft.

At this stage we did not know that suspects were sometimes tried as the result of direct accusation. These are the cases where death or illness in a family are attributed directly to a person who has been "identified" by their next of kin. Such accusations are generally based on old family feuds, personal grievances, or as the result of wagging tongues. The accused person is brought before the village headman or chief where, quite naturally, he stoutly denies all guilt. He is then ordered to submit to the ordeal by poison. The next step is to send for the Mganga, for only he is competent to mix and administer the poison. Since the Mganga is not directly involved in the accusation and the outcome of the ordeal cannot in any way reflect upon his efficiency, he has no particular reason to ensure a fatal termination of the ordeal and it happens quite often that an accused person survives after he has vomited the poison. He is then entitled to claim compensation from his accuser.

But in cases where the Mganga has "found" the culprit the situation is very different. For an accused person to survive the ordeal would be a serious reflection on his ability, and his reputation and dignity will suffer in consequence. He therefore takes every precaution to avoid such an outcome and makes quite certain that the victim will not escape. An accusation by the Mganga is therefore an irrevocable sentence of death and the ensuing ordeal serves only to support that which is already a *fait accompli*. Death from an overdose of Muabvi bark extract, as we were to see the next day, involves the most horrible, appalling suffering imaginable.

Fully an hour before the appointed time the villagers began to arrive at the open square in twos and threes and squatted in a circle. It was a tense hour, heavily charged with dread possibilities for each of them. But such is the absolute faith in the unerring supernatural powers of the witch-doctor that it was not possible to detect any apprehension on the faces of any of the spectators. On the contrary, there was keen anticipation to see a loathsome member of the community exposed and brought to justice.

A few minutes before four o'clock the murmuring sound of voices ceased abruptly as the village headman made his way through the circle of spectators, closely followed by the witch-doctor. Barefooted, and dressed in the gaudy raiment of the members of his profession, the Mganga presented an awesome picture. Around his head he wore a crown of small antelope horns; from a broad leather belt hung numerous pieces of skins —leopard, lion, crocodile, snake, etc., etc., whilst the evil face was further distorted with heavy daubs of charcoal and red ochre paint. In his one hand he carried a small bag which contained the Muabvi bark, in the other he held the heavily ornamented tail of a wildebees. The entire ensemble was obviously designed to give the wearer a truly satanic, fiendish appearance. Following closely behind the Mganga were two natives who carried an elaborate assortment of trappings to be used in the ordeal. These consisted of native pots, calabashes, a live rooster, a bag of small stones, firewood, water, and more skins.

The headman now took up his position in the centre of the circle and announced that a grievous crime had been committed in their midst and called on the victim to come forward and state his case, whereupon a middle-aged native stepped from the circle of spectators and knelt before the Mganga. He went on to explain that his wife, who had always enjoyed good health, had been taken ill recently and died suddenly. His only daughter, who had likewise been in good health, now lay seriously ill and he feared that she, too, would die. He had no doubt that the trouble was due to witchcraft, and as he was unable to determine who was responsible for this evil deed he now appealed to the Mganga for help.

The Mganga's face now assumed an expression of severe gravity. He agreed that it was indeed a case that needed his intervention and immediately proceeded with the work in hand. A fire was lit under an iron plate on which numerous small stones were placed. Water was poured into a calabash and a quantity of powdered bark carefully measured in a cup and emptied into the water. The rooster was then beheaded and a quantity of blood poured into the mixture. The stones on the iron plate were now almost red-hot and these were lifted with a pair of iron tongs and dropped into the calabash containing the mixture until it reached near boiling point. It was then left to cool down.

The Mganga now started to utter a series of weird incantations as he walked round the circle of spectators, closely scrutinizing each individual. As his eyes alighted on a young woman he emitted a loud scream, grabbed her by the arm and led her to the centre of the circle. There she was subjected to a closer examination whilst the weird incantations continued for several seconds. "You are not guilty, my child," exclaimed the old scoundrel in a loud voice as he pushed her roughly from his presence and instructed her to return to her place in the circle. The performance was repeated on several more occasions and by this time the Mganga had worked himself into a frenzy, dancing and jumping like one possessed whilst froth oozed from his mouth. Now he stopped before an aged woman and stared at her. I felt instinctively that the search had come to an end. At his word of command she proceeded to the centre of the circle where, like the others who had preceded her, she was subjected to a close examination. Suddenly we heard a loud, demoniacal scream as the witch-doctor jumped back rapidly as one would from the presence of a poisonous reptile. For a

moment or two he stood looking at the woman with a con-
temptuous sneer on his face and then pointed an accusing finger
at her. The identification was final and complete.

In a pleading, wailing voice the woman protested her innocence, but it was of no avail. The only way for her to *prove* it was
to swallow the draught which the Mganga would measure out
carefully. If she was innocent she would vomit the mixture and
all would be well. If not, she would die the death of a sorceress
and the community would be well rid of her. An enamel mug
was quickly produced into which the Mganga poured a full
pint and ordered her to drink it. Within ten minutes the action
of the poison began to take effect. The victim screamed in agony
and fell to the ground, where she twisted and turned as she tried
desperately to vomit the mixture. It soon became obvious that
she would not succeed and this was the signal for great hilarity
among the spectators, who now crowded in to heap insults and
indignities on the suffering wretch. . . .

This was one of the most callous and barbarous spectacles I
have ever witnessed. I had no doubt whatever that the only
crime this woman had committed was to grow old and un-
attractive. The punishment that was meted out to her was
strictly within keeping of the minds of this horde of savages, but
to heap abuse on the unfortunate creature at a moment when
she was suffering the pangs of hell as death slowly crept over
her, was an inhuman, monstrous crime.

As I stood watching this nauseating spectacle I saw the huge
frame of Micky rushing towards the frantic mob. With revolver
in hand, he quickly scattered them in all directions. For a few
moments he stood looking at the writhing woman and then
walked over to the witch-doctor who stood watching close by.
Under different circumstances I would have left Micky to
handle the old scoundrel in his own way. But we were in a
foreign country and in no position to face the consequences of
an assault on a person who exercised such terrible power over

8

this savage mob of barbarians. I quickly rushed forward and persuaded Micky not to do anything. By this time the woman's movements were becoming more and more feeble. A moment later she uttered a deep guttural moan and lay still. The ritual was over and "justice" had descended upon one more member of an outlawed society.

What we had just witnessed was an unspeakable crime for which I could not find words strong enough in condemnation. But perhaps I was too severe in my strictures, for in the midst of my tirade, Micky, who by now had regained his usual calm, reminded me that it was not so long ago since we ourselves perpetrated similar crimes and meted out even more dreadful punishment to those we found guilty of the crime of sorcery, and even today the Good Book still enjoins us not "to suffer a witch to live".

This was the only occasion on which I actually witnessed an ordeal by poison. Whilst up on the Zambezi River I once declined an invitation to attend a "smelling out" ritual by a witch-doctor of the Barotse tribe. Here the method of "finding" was to submerge the hands of a suspect in boiling water. If the skin peeled off, it was a sign of guilt. The accused person was then hanged head down from a branch of a tree and slowly roasted to death. The fire was kept burning after death until the entrails burst from heat. That was the moment when the evil spirit left the body of the sorcerer. So firmly do they believe in this that their most sacred oath is "on the bursting of the entrails". On taking that oath one felt reasonably certain that the party taking it was as near to telling the truth as he is ever likely to be.

More novel, and less cruel, was the method of yet another Zambezi tribe to establish the virginity of young girls before, and the fidelity of wives after, marriage. To settle such a complex matter the woman is required to take a handful of sand and dive into a river or deep pool of water. If the sand remains

dry after submersion the virginity or fidelity is established beyond all doubt. A hand full of wet sand often has disastrous
consequences. Just how many devoted husbands or lovers have
confused virtue with an ability to close a hand in such a manner
that water will not percolate into the sand it will be difficult to
say.

To return to the ordeal by poison: for the benefit of those of
my readers who have joined in the great crusade for the
"equality" and "advancement" of the African and who believe
that, as a result of their noble efforts, crimes such as I have
described here are no longer perpetrated, I quote from the
Johannesburg *Sunday Times* of August 18th, 1957: "Blantyre
(Nyasaland)—A trial by ordeal—the drinking of Muabvi, a
deadly poison concocted from the bark of the Muabvi tree, is
believed to have caused the deaths of two women near here this
week."

Blantyre is not very far from the place where I saw the
barbarous rite performed.

12

AKKABI TELLS HIS STORY

AFTER I HAD completed my safari in Southern Abyssinia I decided to return south via Kenya. At the time I was ready to start my return journey reports were coming through of considerable activities by Abyssinian raiding parties, and my old friend, Major Darley, with whom I had spent a good deal of time during my stay in the country, thought it would be advisable for me to have the benefit of an experienced guide who knew the country and most of the dialects of its inhabitants. On the Sudan side of the border from which I had entered Abyssinia, things were reasonably calm at the time and such precaution was not necessary, but there were large stretches on the Kenya side where things were very unsettled, and I was glad when the major mentioned to me that he had someone in view who would be able to see me through the most difficult part of my journey. The man to fill the role was Akkabi, an old Somali who had landed in Abyssinia many years earlier, having accompanied an important expedition from Somaliland to Lake Rudolph in the early days.

Akkabi had by that time been in the major's service a number of years and had proved himself a reliable, trustworthy servant and, being possessed of a roving spirit, he was quite willing to accompany me on the trip. Although we encountered none of the bands of raiders on the way, Akkabi's knowledge of the country was of the greatest value to me, and of equal importance and interest were the many stories he had to tell of his experiences on the trip from Somaliland to Lake Rudolph. The expedition he accompanied did the trip towards the end of the 'nineties and consisted of several Europeans. It was, by all accounts, one of the first ever to reach Lake Rudolph from Somaliland, and the expedition had many encounters with hostile Abyssinian tribes and saw the appalling suffering of the Gallas at the hands of these savages. These events have been dealt with exhaustively by writers who visited Abyssinia in later years. But Akkabi's stories about his adventures with the expedition fall in a different category and are of sufficient interest to record.

"The white man who was in charge of the expedition from Somaliland was a doctor and a very strange man," said Akkabi. "He had three other Europeans with him and also one hundred and forty natives. It needed more than a hundred camels to carry all his equipment for he had many strange instruments with which he measured the country and looked at the stars at night. He had nearly a hundred rifles with him, fifteen large cases full of ammunition and a great many cases of tinned foods and medicines. There were many other cases in which he put all the different kinds of insects, birds, lizards and snakes he collected on the way.

"All the Europeans were keen on hunting, but they had done very little hunting before and it took us quite a long time to teach them the ways of the bush. It was in the beginning when they were still learning that they had so many narrow escapes and lost one man to a bull elephant. Apart from the white man who was killed by the elephant, we also lost four natives to dangerous animals, and many of us who accompanied the expedition had very narrow escapes.

"If you will look at my back and see the scars I have there you will understand what I mean. This is what happened to me one afternoon when one of them wounded a rhino and missed his second shot when the bull charged. There was only one tree close to us and the white man made for it. I was waiting for him to climb high enough so that I may also get out of the bull's reach, but I never had time to start climbing before he got me. This big scar on my legs is where the horn entered when he tossed me. I landed on my face several yards from him and he came for me again. The marks on my back are where he scraped me with his horn when he tried to lift me again. It was lucky for me that the rhino is such a stupid beast; because his horn always points upwards he is not able to lift a person lying flat on the ground so easily and he never thinks of stamping one to death with his heavy front feet like elephants and buffaloes do. After I had been lying there for some time with the bull standing over me grunting and blowing off steam as he kept rubbing my back with his horn, I heard a shot. The bull immediately left me, walked a few yards and fell down dead. If he had hooked me in the stomach or chest I would have been killed instantly.

"After the accident I was carried back to camp where the doctor stitched up the wounds and attended to them daily until I was cured.

"Rhinos were very plentiful in those parts and we had lots of trouble with them. One morning a cow charged the column of camels; one of the Europeans shot her in the shoulder and she rolled over, but she quickly got up again, rushed at the leading camel and dug her horn deep into its stomach and then fell down dead. The camel had to be destroyed for all its entrails were protruding from the hole where the horn had entered.

"Yet another morning I was at the head of the column of porters when a big bull suddenly appeared in the road a few yards ahead of us. He snorted and blew off steam loudly. I had no gun with me and expected him to kill me any moment, but he suddenly turned off into the bush and made a great noise as he ran away from us. A few hundred yards farther he was again standing facing us and started to walk towards us. When he was only a few yards from us he again ran into the bush, and we had not walked far when we met him again standing in the road and blowing steam. This time he looked very angry and we all rushed for the trees, but while we were busy climbing he suddenly ran off and we never saw him again. Just why he did not charge us I do not know, but the porters were so scared they threw down their loads in all directions as they made for the trees and it took us a long time to collect all the loads again after the bull had disappeared for the last time.

"Crocodiles also gave us a lot of trouble. One morning when we were busy carrying sheep across a river a big brute got hold of one of the porters by his arm and started to pull him down into the water. The other natives quickly came to his aid and pulled at his other arm. This went on for quite a time before some natives from the other bank of the river came along with their spears and killed the croc. The boy's arm was so badly injured that the doctor had to cut it off at the shoulder a few minutes later. Then another croc got hold of a pack mule one morning. There was a terrible struggle when the natives closed in to try and rescue the mule. One native was drowned and the mule had to be destroyed. When we pulled the croc out of the water there were more than a hundred spears sticking in his body. He was an enormous creature.

"Then there was the morning when we saw two elephants in a plain about five hundred yards away. The safari was halted whilst the European in charge walked over to have a shot. He got quite close to the animals before he fired and wounded the bull. The elephant screamed loudly and immediately charged. A second shot had no effect on him and a moment later the man was lifted high into the air on the bull's trunk. For nearly a minute he stood swinging the man in the air and then smashed him down on the ground; after that he started to trample the victim with his front feet. We were too far away to help in any way but after the bull had left we went over to the spot where the accident had occurred. The man's body was as flat as a piece of paper and we put it into a sack and carried it to the next camp where we buried him the following morning.

"Another morning I was walking on a path with one of the other Europeans; we were quite two miles ahead of the column when we saw a small herd of elephants. We crawled within thirty yards of them when the European fired and dropped a big bull. We went over to examine the tusks and the elephant appeared to be quite dead. As the rest of the herd had not gone far, the European followed them and told me to remain with the dead animal. I was sitting on top of the elephant when it suddenly started moving. A moment later he was standing up erect and I was hiding behind a small tree. I fired two shots at him with the double-barrel rifle and hit in the shoulder on both occasions, but he took no notice of me at all and kept on walking away slowly. As I had no more ammunition I remained at the spot, and when the European returned an hour later he found me waiting there for him to tell him what had happened. We spent the rest of the day looking for the elephant but never saw him again.

"One night when we were in bad lion country we tied a donkey to a tree for bait and built a small zariba close to it. Shortly after dark the doctor and I went and sat inside the zariba to wait for the lions to come and take the bait. There was only a half moon and it must have been after midnight when we heard a terrific snarl, and this was followed by a heavy thud as the lion jumped on the donkey and knocked it down. The lion was standing over the donkey when the doctor fired. There was a loud roar when the bullet struck him, and the next moment a big shadow came rushing towards us and jumped on top of the zariba. When the lion landed on top of it the whole lot collapsed on top of us—lion and all. For a few minutes we lay there without making a movement, but when we found that the lion was not making an attempt to get at us we crawled out cautiously from underneath him. He was lying dead on the spot where he had landed. When we examined him we found that he had been shot through the heart.

"The strangest and most exciting thing I ever saw in the bush was the night when we put out a hartebeest carcass for bait and tied a sick donkey next to it. We again built a zariba near by and the doctor and I sat up waiting for lions. It was a bright, moonlight night and we had not been there long before we could hear hyenas in the distance. Suddenly we were aware of lions quite close to us. A moment later a lion was crouching right up against the zariba; he was so close to us we could hear his heavy breathing as he crawled past us towards the bait. It was a terrible moment, for the zariba was constructed so that only a small opening faced the bait. It was not only impossible but much too dangerous to shoot from such a short distance, so we both sat still—not daring to breathe loudly.

"We were still sitting trembling with fear in case the lion should suddenly turn on us when all hell was let loose as a pack of at least fifty hyenas attacked the lions. It was the most fearful, blood-curdling noise I have ever heard in the bush. The hyenas were growling and snarling as loudly as the lions, of which there were five. People say that hyenas are cowards and will not attack anything that can defend itself, but that is not always true. Not one of those hyenas was a coward and they attacked as savagely as the lions did. This terrible fight would have lasted until one side or the other had won, but the doctor foolishly spoiled the show when a big lion with his mane raised stood a few yards from us and he fired at it. A second later the fight was at an end and we could hear the growls and grunts as the animals ran off into the bush. When we got out of the zariba the lion at which the doctor had fired was nowhere to be seen. Close to us two hyenas were lying kicking and grunting, and these we killed. In those days we did not have shooting lamps like you have now and we went back to camp and retired for the night.

"Early the next morning we went out to see the results of the previous night's battle. We found another hyena lying dead a few yards from the zariba and the donkey was still standing where we had tied it. All over the grass there were heavy blood trails and this made it impossible to tell which was the trail of the wounded lion. But we called out all the porters with their pangas and spears and got them to surround every patch of grass and scrub in the vicinity until at last we came to a patch of grass where the lion had taken cover. The porters kept on shouting and beating their drums until at last the lion made a dash for safety. As he jumped out of the grass one of the porters failed to get out of his way quickly enough and the lion knocked him down. It was as he started to pull the man apart that the other natives closed in on him and speared him to death. We found afterwards that he had a fractured front leg where the doctor had shot him the night before. He was an enormous beast with a big black mane, but the skin was completely spoiled by the many spear cuts. The head and the mane were not damaged, and the doctor took these back to camp.

"After the lion was killed we followed blood spoors for long distances in all directions but we never saw any more lions or hyenas. If the doctor had not fired that shot I am sure there would have been a fight to a finish that night, and from the manner in which the hyenas attacked I am quite certain they would have won, for there were at least ten of them for each lion.

"You may think that what I have told you about this lion–hyena fight is not the truth, but I assure you that every word is true. These things do happen in the bush, and when I told the major about it he was not surprised, for he had himself seen the same thing happen on the Sudanese border.

"A short time after this we were attacked by a party of over one thousand natives of the Boran tribe. We were lucky that it happened in day-time otherwise we would all have been killed. All three Europeans and more than seventy Somali gun-bearers opened fire on the Borans who were armed with bows and arrows. After two volleys had been fired they ran away, but they left fourteen dead behind. These people were very stupid to attack us, for a few days later we caught two of their scouts and for the first time they realized that we were not Abyssinian bandits. The doctor gave these men a lot of presents of beads and mirrors and sent them back to their chief.

"The next day the chief came with six warriors; they all carried long green branches in their hands; this was a sign that they wanted peace. The doctor ordered them to come to his tent, where the chief explained that it was all a mistake. Later in the day he sent over some goats and sheep as well as four fat oxen to show his regrets for what had happened. We traded a lot of sheep and goats with them and continued our journey towards Lake Stephanie.

"Before we got to the lake we came across a strange tribe of pygmies. They were completely wild and lived like animals. Neither the men nor the women wore any clothes at all, and they had never seen Europeans before. They had a great many ivory tusks and lots of carved bracelets. For an empty jam or milk tin they were willing to give one elephant tusk in ex-change. The tins they cut up into squares which they tied to their noses so as to cover their mouths. These people belonged to the Dume tribe; they were very small but I do not believe there are any more of them left, for they were regularly raided by the Abyssinians and other tribes, and when we passed their way they told us there were only a few hundred of their tribe left.

"When we finally arrived at Lake Rudolph we had been on the road for a full year. I returned with the expedition for only a short distance, for we heard that there was heavy fighting going on between the Abyssinians and the Gallas and I did not think it would be safe to pass through that part of the country again. I do not know whether the Europeans ever got back to this country again or whether they were killed by the Abyssinians. I have forgotten now what the name of the doctor was who was in charge of the expedition. It happened a long long time ago and I was very young at the time."

There were a number of things in Akkabi's story that puzzled me. The elephant that walked off quietly whilst lead was being pumped into him seemed strange to me, but it is quite possible that the animal was so badly stunned or blinded that it did not realize just what was happening to it. The Dume pygmies also seem to have vanished for good as no one in those parts knew anything about them. A few stray members of the tribe may have been absorbed by other friendly tribes nearby.

The story about the hyena–lion fight was the most puzzling of all, for I had never heard of a similar occurrence before. But, as Akkabi told me that Major Darley knew of a similar case, I determined to write to him about it. In reply to my letter he stated that it was quite true. A pack of hyenas, numbering about twelve, were attacked by two lions—male and female. The hyenas did not retreat as they usually do on such occasions but put up a fight which lasted about ten minutes. The lion was first to retire from the battle and the female followed him. Here also, two hyenas were killed, but he could not tell what damage was done to the lions as it happened at night whilst he was watching a bait he had put out. After the fight the hyenas returned to the kill and finished the remains. "In view of their plucky fight I did not disturb them but left them to clean up the rest of the bait," his letter concluded. All of which goes to show that there is no telling how animals will react under different circumstances. Extreme hunger may have been responsible in both these cases, as I do not think that hyenas will ever defy a lion in the ordinary course of events.

I have never been able to find out the name of the expedition with which Akkabi made his adventurous journey, but I believe that the Smithsonian Mission once had an expedition out in that part of the world.

13

ECHOES OF THE PAST

W HEN THE LATE King Albert visited the Belgian Congo in 1928, I was a member of the organizing committee during his stay in Jadotville, where he was due to perform a number of public duties. One of these was to present a large plot of farming land to a certain "Boetie" Adams. This grant from the Belgian Government was in recognition of the fact that Boetie was at the time the oldest white settler in the Belgian Congo, having arrived there in the early 'nineties.

During the course of the ceremony I was introduced to Boetie —one of the strangest characters I have ever met in Central Africa. He was then a man well in his seventies. Boetie had come to the Katanga via Uganda, on his way to the Kivu where he intended to hunt the gorilla—or, if possible—to capture a baby or two.

At the time of our meeting I was operating a catering contract for the Union Miniere, the great mining company of the Congo, and during his stay at Jadotville, I provided accommodation for Boetie. In the few short conversations I had with him it was quite obvious that, like all other pioneers of that time, he had a fund of adventure stories to tell; but owing to the rush of work, I had neither the time nor the opportunity to talk to him about his adventurous past. After the festivities were over, I lost sight of him, and it was nearly two years later when he called on me at my office one morning. The two intervening years had not dealt too kindly with Boetie. His attempt to develop the land he had received from the government had absorbed all his available capital and he was at a loose end, looking for something to do to keep the wolf from the door.

It was quite a normal thing for men who were down on their luck at the time to call on me and ask for food and shelter until they were able to find work and once more depend on their own resources. In Boetie's case, I was quite content to come to the rescue, but owing to his advanced age the tide was a long time turning in his favour, and during the months that followed I often sat listening to him at night when he told of his many strange adventures. Although the setting was not strictly a camp-fire scene, it was only the circumstances that prevented it from being so, and, as I have done in other cases, I am falling back on my diaries to record the most interesting part of Boetie's story:

"I passed through Uganda on my way to Ruwenzori at the time the British Government was having trouble with King Kabarega, one of the most powerful and savage native kings of that period. It must have been a great relief to his many chiefs when he was finally driven from the country, for whatever advantages they may have enjoyed in their exalted positions were completely offset when the king held his annual assembly of chiefs. On these occasions they would gather in a big square near the palace and form a circle. The king would walk round this circle and greet each chief in a cordial manner, after which he would select one at random and invite him to the centre of the circle where the unfortunate man was promptly beheaded in full view of the assembly. The blood was caught in a bowl and sprinkled in all directions, after which the body was thrown out for the hyenas and vultures to devour.

"It was atrocities such as these, and the fact that he was for ever busy stirring up trouble, that prompted the British Government to expel him from the country. It was when the trouble was at its height that I passed through the country and Kabarega was too occupied with his other troubles to worry about me and my safari of eighty porters and bodyguard of six armed natives, and we passed through his country without serious molestation until we came near Lake George. There we had a spot of bother when four of my native porters failed to arrive in camp one night. I had a feeling that there was trouble brewing and early the next morning we went back on the trail to look for them. After we had walked for an hour we came to a cluster of dense bush and beneath a big tree we found the remains of the four men. Their bodies were horribly mutilated and in each case the head had been cut off at the shoulders and taken away. Of the loads they had carried there was no sign to be seen.

"The natives there, as everywhere else, have an uncanny way of finding out things in the bush, and it was not long before they reported to me that the person responsible for the outrage was a village chief about two hours' walk from our camp. We immediately set out for this place and arrived there shortly after midday. The chief was an arrogant, insolent native, and through an interpreter he demanded to know what I was doing at his village. I told him that I had come for an explanation for the attack on my porters and to collect the loads he had stolen. In reply, he told me that he had no explanation to give me and that he knew nothing about my loads. Furthermore, it was his desire that I should quit the vicinity immediately or take the consequences if I failed to do so.

"I was still busy telling him that I had no intention of returning without my loads when he grabbed a spear. As he lifted his arm to throw it at me I sent a pistol bullet through his shoulder and the spear fell harmlessly at his side. A dozen or more warriors who had been watching proceedings from a nearby hut suddenly made a rush for us. I shouted at them to halt, but they ignored my order. A second later four of them lay on the ground with bullets through their legs. That seemed to bring them to their senses and they stopped abruptly. It was a tense moment though, for from all sides the villagers began to crowd in on us, but they soon retreated when they saw the six men of my bodyguard raising their rifles to their shoulders. I ordered them all to retire to the far end of the village whilst we started to search the huts for my belongings. Most of the goods were stacked in the chief's hut, and after removing them I set the place alight. After that we searched the other huts systematically and burned down every one in which we found goods hidden.

"On our way back to camp we were followed by warriors from the village who took cover in the bush and shot arrows at us. The trouble stopped when we took up our position on the top of a big ant-hill and hid behind some scrub. After we had picked off a few of their marksmen from a long distance they decided that their bows and arrows were not a match for our rifles and they left us to go our way without further molestation. We had no more trouble with the tribesmen during the rest of our trip through this part of the country, but I had many exciting adventures in the bush, for I intended to collect as much ivory as possible on this safari. Game was exceedingly plentiful and big tuskers were not difficult to find.

"One afternoon I went out with a few spotters and gun-bearers and we soon picked up the trail of a big elephant herd which we followed into dense forest. As we were walking along cautiously on the trail we heard the rumbling of an elephant's stomach. Whilst we were creeping slowly in the direction of the sound we suddenly heard stomachs rumbling behind us and at our side. The herd had scattered whilst feeding and we had landed ourselves in the middle of them. In the dense bush and long grass it was quite impossible to tell just where we might find an opening to escape from the herd, and I decided the best thing to do would be to creep as near as possible to the one in front of us and, if possible, to get him out of the way with a brain shot.

9

"A few yards farther on I saw an enormous bull with a pair of outsize tusks. There was no doubt he was the bull we had heard first. I sat down and took careful aim for a spot between his ear and the eye. Immediately the shot rang out there was pandemonium all round us and the herd of at least fifty animals started screaming and trumpeting simultaneously. In every direction we could hear branches and trees crashing down as the herd kept milling round us. Just how we managed to escape being trampled to death by the infuriated animals I will never understand. The long grass and dense undergrowth provided good cover and we all remained flat on our stomachs, crawling foot by foot, until nearly an hour later we managed to escape from the danger zone. It was certainly one of the most unpleasant hours I have ever spent in the bush, for during that time several members of the herd passed within a few feet of me—each with its trunk raised high and squealing loudly. By the time we were out of danger the sun was ready to set and we decided to get back to camp and return early the next morning to search for the bull I had fired at. I had seen it go down after my shot, but with all the confusion which followed I could not tell whether it was only a temporary collapse or whether I had scored a brain shot.

"Early the next morning we were once again back on the trail. We soon found the spot where I had dropped the bull, and from there we followed a heavy blood spoor for several miles before we again spotted the herd standing sleeping in dense forest. Close to us was a big ant-hill and this we decided to mount so as to be able to survey the herd in reasonable safety in the hopes of seeing the wounded bull. After we had been there for more than an hour they started moving about and it was not difficult to identify the wounded animal. He was then quite eighty yards from me, but after the experience of the previous day, I decided to take a shot at long range rather than risk another encounter with the herd. This time I aimed for the heart and a moment after I had fired there was once again a wild stampede as they rushed about the bush screaming and trumpeting. As on the previous day, we could hear trees and branches crashing all over and the noise was terrifying.

"A few minutes later they all grouped together; one big bull was venting his spleen by pulling up grass by its roots and tossing it over his shoulder. Every now and again a few members of the herd would walk a few yards from the group and sniff the air in an attempt to pick up our scent which, luckily, they failed to do as the wind was in our favour. After each unsuccessful attempt they returned and grouped again with the others. This continued for more than half an hour and then they started to move off deeper into the bush—that is, all but four, who remained behind and walked in circles round the spot where they had previously grouped. On closely watching this position we finally spotted the big bull lying down, but it was not possible to tell whether he was still alive. It was fully an hour later before they vacated the scene and we were able to go down and investigate and found the bull quite dead. The tusks were even better than I had expected and the two together weighed a little under 300 lb. I left the natives to chop out the tusks and dissect the carcass whilst I went back to camp to send porters to carry in the meat.

"I had not been back in camp more than ten minutes when one of the natives whom I had left at the carcass came rushing in to tell me that whilst they were busy cutting out the tusks a cow had suddenly appeared on the scene. There was a wild scramble to get out of her way, but she had caught one of the porters and the last he had seen was the man dangling in her trunk high above her head. I set out at once to the scene of the trouble and, taking advantage of the wind, I was able to approach within thirty yards of where the bull was lying. There was no sign of the cow and I was just about to walk over to the carcass when I noticed a movement ahead of me. A moment later she came out into the open with her trunk raised high and her ears flapping. It was obvious that she was suspicious and ready to cause more trouble. When she came near to the carcass she became greatly agitated, and whilst she was busy stamping on the ground with her front feet I placed a bullet in her brain. The effect was instantaneous, and as she fell down in a kneeling position her tusks all but touched the dead bull. Not far from her lay the remains of the porter; not only had she flattened him out completely, but she had also torn his limbs from the body and scattered them. Among the dangerous animals it is strange, but true, that the female is generally the more vindictive killer; the notable exception is in the case of buffaloes, for it is rare indeed for a cow to attack, and when she does she is generally satisfied to horn her victim to death and leave it at that.

"We left this camp the next morning on our way to Lake Edward. In this region I had some of my most exciting adventures with lions. I believe that they are more numerous there than in any other part of Central Africa. When we arrived at a village one morning the natives received us with open arms and the old headman was soon telling me about the trouble they were having with man-eaters. Only two days before our arrival one of them had visited the village for the third time in one week. That night he had forced his way into a hut and grabbed one of the sleeping natives. The man was sleeping under a strip of tarpaulin and a heavy blanket, and to this fact he owed his life, for the lion in its hurry had departed with the tarpaulin and blanket and left a badly frightened native behind.

"As one story of lion depravity followed another my natives decided that this was no place for us to remain and insisted that we make for a camp on the other side of a river some ten miles away. We arrived there late in the afternoon after crossing a stream shoulder high in water. By sunset we had a small enclosure ready for the few goats we had with us and several big fires were burning. Later in the evening the fires were stacked up with big piles of wood and the natives prepared for bed, feeling certain that with ten miles and a running stream of water between us and the man-eater, they would be quite safe for the night. Before turning in later I went out twice to make sure that all was well and found the watchman on duty and the rest of the gang fast asleep. At 2 a.m. I was awakened by loud screams and shouts of Simba, Simba, and saw logs of fire flying in all directions. I quickly grabbed my rifle and rushed out on the trail of the shouting natives. Two hundred yards from camp we found a man lying unconscious. His leg was badly lacerated where the lion had seized him and he had several other injuries on his chest and arms, but luckily no bones were broken. When he regained consciousness he told us how he was awakened when the lion seized him and how he had grabbed the beast round its neck and hung on whilst he shouted on the top of his voice. With the other natives in pursuit, screaming and throwing burning logs and spears, the lion had dropped him and disappeared in the bush; a moment later all 'went black' and he remembered nothing else.

"The man was carried back to camp where I attended to his injuries and bathed the open wounds with a strong solution of permanganate of potash. For the rest of the night everything remained quiet but for the talking and murmuring of the gang. As I had decided to remain in this vicinity some time to hunt ivory, I got all the natives busy the next day to erect pole and grass huts for themselves. That night, and also the next night, there was no further trouble, and by this time the huts had been properly reinforced. The following night there was a clear sky and a full moon was shining brightly. After the heavy rains of the two previous days the air was stifling and I decided to sleep in the open under my mosquito net. Shortly after mid-night I was aroused by the loud bleating of the goats near my tent. As I opened my eyes and looked round in a half sleep I stared into the face of a big male lion standing next to me and looking at me intently. Had it not been for the mosquito net covering me I am convinced he would not have wasted time looking at the unfamiliar object hanging over me. The shock was so great and paralysing that I let out a mighty yell before I could move to grab my rifle on the ground next to me. When I looked round again, rifle in hand, the lion was gone.

"The place was definitely becoming unhealthy, for there was no way of telling whether there was more than one lion responsible for these raids. But I was doing very well at ivory hunting and made up my mind to remain in the area for at least another week. The next night we were left in peace, but shortly after breakfast a native from the village ten miles away came in to report that yet another man had been taken during the night and begged me to move camp closer to the village so as to sit up at night and wait for the marauder. My natives, however, were by now all in a panic of fear and wanted none of such a scheme, in fact, they insisted that we should vacate the district as soon as possible. But this I could not do imme-diately, for on the previous day I had shot two elephants and wounded a big bull. This happened late in the afternoon and we had not the time to collect the ivory and meat. I finally persuaded them to postpone our departure until the ivory of the two dead animals was recovered and also to allow me time to go after the big bull I had wounded. As soon as all this was attended to I promised them we could move on to healthier parts.

"The next day I left some men to attend to the two elephants I had shot the previous day whilst along with a few trackers and spotters I set out after the wounded bull. It was shortly before sunset when I caught up with him and brought him down with a shot in the heart. We were more than ten miles from camp and it was after nine o'clock before we got back that night. Once again we slept peacefully and early the next morning I took a gang of natives to collect the ivory and meat of the last kill. Cutting out the tusks and preparing the loads of meat took best part of the day, and we landed back in camp just before sunset.

"That night we also slept in peace and the next morning I was busy giving instructions to break camp when a native came in to report a big bull elephant close by. That upset all the arrangements for a move that day, for I decided to go after the bull. We soon got on his trail and he must have been an enormous animal, judging by his tracks. The luck, however, went against us and a full day's trailing brought us no results, and when we got back to camp that night I instructed the natives to prepare everything for a move early the next morning. When we turned in that night none of us anticipated the serious trouble which awaited us only a few hours later.

"The fires were burning brightly and everything was quiet except for hyenas calling in the distance. At 2 a.m. I got out of bed and had a walk round; a heavy drizzle had set in, but for the rest, the world was at peace—a peace that was rudely disturbed less than an hour later when loud screams and shouts from the largest of the native huts awakened me. I quickly rushed out with my rifle in hand, ready for action. A few yards from the door of the hut whence came the screaming I found a group of natives gathered round a man lying on the ground. It did not need a second look to tell me that he was beyond all help, for the whole of his throat had been torn away. The natives explained that the lion had forced its way through the grass wall, grabbed the sleeping man and dragged him through a small opening. They had immediately rushed after it with spears and burning faggots. As a result of this hot reception the lion had dropped the man where he was now lying. For the remaining two hours of darkness there was no peace as the natives sat talking and wailing over their dead brother.

"When daylight came we made the necessary preparations to bury the dead man, and after that we held a council of war. I told the gang that I was determined to remain where we were and settle the score with the marauder. After a great deal of arguing and talking, during which I explained my plan to them, it was agreed that we should remain. My plan, in short, was to erect a drop door box trap a hundred yards from camp in which a goat would be tied for bait. The camp-fires were to be kept burning brightly throughout the night, and for this purpose they would have to keep watch for three shifts whilst two armed men would be on duty on each shift. That night the trap was ready and the goat securely tied inside it; but the lion did not put in an appearance. The next two nights also passed without incident. On the third night a steady rain set in shortly after sunset. It is on dark, rainy nights that lions are more active than usual, and I had a feeling that the raider would visit us before daylight next morning. Instructions were given to the watchmen to pay particular attention to the fires, which were protected from the rain by rough grass roofing. By talking loudly and occasionally beating a drum it was more or less certain that they would keep the brute away from camp, and if he was hungry the bleating goat would attract his attention. For the next two hours the drum was beaten incessantly and the entire camp was lit up. It was in the midst of all this noise that we suddenly heard loud snarling and grunting whilst the goat bleated louder than ever.

"In a few moments the entire camp was astir. With burning logs and a hurricane lamp to light the way, we rushed over to the bait, and there, crouching in the corner of the trap, baring her fangs and snarling viciously at us, sat a full-grown female. The trap was especially well constructed with heavy logs and there was not the slightest chance of her breaking it down or escaping. In spite of her savage growls, which had now reached a crescendo, the natives kept shouting and dancing and hurling insults at the infuriated beast. It was when they started to push burning sticks at her through the crevices of the walls that I decided to call a halt to proceedings and sent a bullet through her brain.

"We left this camp the following day, knowing full well that we had eliminated only part of the trouble, for that big male that stood looking at me through the mosquito net that night was still at large, and who knows, there might have been several others who had taken a liking to the taste of human flesh.

"Two weeks later we were at the foot of the great Ruwenzori mountain. I remained there for a full month looking for gorillas but I never saw one, for the conditions were all against us. I did, however, hear the nocturnal chorus of Ruwenzori ghosts high up in the mountain—the most eerie, blood-curdling sound in all Africa. Shortly after dark the first weird call could be heard and the echo was much worse than the call itself. A few minutes later the call is taken up higher in the mountain cliffs and before long the shrill, unearthly sounds could be heard on all sides—a veritable devil's chorus, the kind of thing Dante must have had in mind when he wrote the *Inferno*. The natives believe that it is the God of the Mountain who sends forth the ghosts at night to warn trespassers of his disapproval. It may even be so, for during the time I spent there I never saw an animal or any other living creature that could be capable of making such demoniacal sounds. It was the first time in my life that I really feared the unknown and that was the main reason why I abandoned my search for the gorilla and turned south again."

Boetie had many more exciting adventures to relate about his trip down the lakes on native canoes. On Lake Tanganyika he lost all his belongings when the canoe sank and he escaped death by a miracle and lived on wild fruits and fish for three weeks.

Three months after Boetie arrived to stay with me at Jadot-ville, he came to me and informed me that he had secured a contract on excavation work in the Ruwe goldfield—one of the richest gold-bearing areas in the Katanga. A few days later we parted company and I did not expect ever to see him again. It was nearly a year later when a smart chauffeur-driven limousine pulled up outside my office. In the back seat, im-maculately dressed in a perfectly tailored suit, and showing unmistakable signs of prosperity, sat my old friend, Boetie. A moment later we adjourned to the lounge, where he told me that he had "struck it rich". He had just returned from Johannesburg where he had settled some "important business" and he was now on his way back north. His main reason for calling on me was to settle his little account in respect of board and lodging. It so happened that I never opened an account for Boetie and I explained this to him. A little later we bade each other adieu for the last time. The next morning a messenger from the bank delivered a letter to me; it contained a credit slip for a substantial amount paid in to my account by Buton C. Adams. At the very least, it exceeded by ten times the amount he could possibly have owed me.

It was only after this practical demonstration of affluence that I began to think things over and remembered that a Greek, who also had an excavation contract on the same stretch of country as Boetie, had been arrested on the Congo-Rhodesian border a few months earlier with a trunk full of alluvial gold. As Boetie was engaged on similar work in the same area, it would not be stretching the imagination too far if I attribute his sudden wealth to a more successful method of handling illicit gold from the Ruwe district.

A little more than a year later an obituary notice appeared in the *Essor du Congo* in Elisabethville. Boetie Adams, the oldest white settler in the Katanga, had departed for the Land of No Return.

The chorus of the Ruwenzori ghosts to which Boetie referred is believed to be the night calls of hyraxes which inhabit the inaccessible cliffs in the middle and upper heights of the great mountain range. In appearance these animals resemble large guinea-pigs. They are seldom, if ever, seen by day owing to the dense vegetation and bad visibility in those regions.

14

JUMBOS AND JU-JUS

IN MY previous book, *African Adventures*, I devoted a chapter to the strange ability of natives in Central Africa to relay correct information by means of drums—a fact which is still disputed in certain quarters today.

When I was hunting on the Lomami River in the Belgian Congo, my headman came to me one morning and told me that they had received messages the previous night to say that there was another European hunting higher up the river. He had quite a lot of information to give me about this European who, he stated, had been in the district a long time. But on the point which interested me the most—the distance to this European's camp—he was unable to furnish any reliable information. It was once again a case of *Mbali Kidogo*, which, when literally translated, means a "little bit far", but in actual fact may mean anything from one to one thousand miles. I had, however, sufficient confidence in drum-communicated messages to believe the story and kept on reminding them regularly about my eagerness to meet this person, for in the part of the country where I was operating it was a very rare occurrence to encounter other safaris in those days.

It was a fortnight later, and quite two hundred miles farther along the river when my safari landed near a place named Etoka, where I met Harry MacCleod—an elderly Scot who, as my headman had told me previously, had been in that part of the country for a considerable time. Harry, in fact, had been in those parts for a good many years and was at that moment

carrying on a very lucrative business which consisted not only
of hunting, but also of trading ivory—mostly illicit—from the
natives. This ivory he ingeniously transported by means of
porters and native canoes to a place named Isangi at the con-
fluence of the Lomami and Congo Rivers, from where it was
taken to Leopoldville where, many years previously, he had
evolved a successful method of disposing of his wares without
too much official interference.

In his search for "easy ivory" before he had concluded the
present satisfactory arrangement, Harry had at various times
operated in the Middle (French) Congo, Gabon, and had even
gone as far afield as the Cameroons and Southern Nigeria. Like
myself, he had passed through the Ubangi cannibal country,
and on his travels farther north he had seen enough of the savage
tribes and their customs to fill a large volume. I remained with
him for the best part of a month, and during that period the
camp-fire often burned late into the night as he sat telling me
of his many experiences on the trail of "easy ivory".

"Amongst the strangest of savages I ever met in the Congo,"
he told me one night, "were the Bambaras, Bayakas and
Bayanzis, who all live along the Ubangi River. As you know,
they are all cannibal tribes, but that is a matter of little importance. What interested me far more was their strange and
savage customs. Among the Bambaras, for instance, the chief
of a district often sent out a raiding party, and when they
returned they were obliged to hand over to him all the ribs of
the people they had killed on the expedition. Human ribs being
a special delicacy, the common folk were allowed to eat it only
by consent of the chief. In order to provide for the proceeds of
a successful raid, a large hut was kept in readiness for storage
purposes. The fact that the flesh sometimes became a bit 'high'
during storage did not detract from its value; in fact, the
'higher' the flesh, the better they seemed to like it.

"Like all other savages, most of their disputes and quarrels are settled—even today—by *putu*, the poison ordeal. This poison also is taken from the bark of a tree; it is mixed with maize meal, and the accused person is ordered to eat four or five small loaves at intervals of about five minutes. The result is always one of three things: the victim dies, which proves him guilty and that settles the matter; he vomits the concoction, which proves him innocent and he is then carried triumphantly around the village on the shoulders of his friends and his accuser pays him a pig or a goat in compensation. If the poison is purged and the victim survives, the verdict is somewhat on the lines of 'not proven', as we have it in Scotland. But that is where the similarity ends, for in Scotland such a verdict secures an acquittal; in Bambaraland the doubtful culprit is taken into the bush where he is made to dig a grave for himself. On completing the job he is served with a cooked rooster, which he eats. The meal is washed down with large quantities of palm wine; in fact, the man drinks until he is completely drunk, and he is then laid in the grave he has dug and covered with earth. A fire is made on the mound and kept burning night and day for two days, after which the corpse is exhumed and eaten by the rest of the community.

"The Bayakas again, although cannibals, will eat anything in the meat line, but they draw the line at dogs, and under no circumstances whatever is a woman allowed to eat fowls or eggs. They may not even cook their food in a pot in which a fowl has been cooked previously. Among the men a hen may be shared with others, but a rooster must be eaten by one man only. Thus, when a child is born, the father kills a rooster and sprinkles the blood over the newly born babe. After that he sits down and eats the rooster by himself. For twelve months after the birth of the child neither the father nor the child is allowed to wash; the mother is kept in seclusion during that period.

"I landed at a Bayaka village one morning with the meat larder completely dry. For some reason game was extremely scarce in the district, but fish, I was told, was plentiful in a nearby river. Soon after we had pitched camp I opened my provisions boxes and got out some fish hooks, one of which I gave to the chief. It was the first time he had ever seen a proper fish hook and he was very much taken up with it. A short while later we were installed on the bank of the river. Fish appeared to be plentiful, but there was no suitable bait available. I was busy digging into the bank of the river, looking for worms, when there was a loud cry by one of the piccaninnies. That youngster had every reason to scream, for the old chief had grabbed him by the ear and cut it off with his hunting knife. A moment later he offered me a piece of the ear for bait. It was the first time I had ever used human ears for bait, but I must admit that the results were very satisfactory indeed.

"Before I left the village next day I traded a number of hooks with the chief. I never returned to that village so I am not able to say how many of the villagers lost their ears in order to keep the hooks properly baited.

"Natives, as a rule, are dirty in their personal habits, but I think the dirtiest race on earth are the Bayanzis, north of Stanley Pool in the Belgian Congo. Like their neighbours, they are also cannibals, and like many other cannibal tribes in Central Africa, they practise cannibalism, not so much because they are always meat hungry, but because they consider human flesh better and tastier than any other. But that does not prevent them from eating any and every other kind of meat— even in the last stages of putrefaction. The day after I arrived at one of their small villages I shot a big bull elephant. The entire village promptly turned out to collect the meat which was stored in a hut beside the chief's and to which he alone had access, and from there he issued rations daily to the community. The climate there is so hot and humid that meat will not keep for more than a day, but when I left the village ten days later the old chief was still busy distributing elephant meat daily to his people. By that time I found it impossible to approach within a hundred yards of the hut for the smell, and the entire place was besieged by millions of blue flies. But still there was a wild rush for a share of the spoils when the store-room was opened in the mornings.

"In spite of their craving for human flesh, the Bayanzis will not eat a person who has died from natural causes. This has nothing to do with hygiene, they believe that the spirit of such a person will come back and harm them. This, of course, is something in their favour. Another of their customs that may be worthy of consideration by more enlightened people, is their law in regard to married women. Their morals, as may be expected, are not entirely beyond reproach, and a prospective husband does not take the trouble to inquire too closely into the character of his future wife. It is only when she finds herself pregnant that her past comes up for consideration, for she is then required to confess all her former lovers to her husband. There is a great deal of importance attached to this confession, for the omission of any one of those who had previously enjoyed her favours will bring death to the child of the marriage. The husband is not unduly upset by the confession—however long the list may be, for immediately after the confession he rounds up all the paramours and collects a suitable present from each of them. Those who have shared the lady's favours after marriage pay a little more.

"In spite of their unenviable reputation, I went through the Bayanzie country without any trouble. This may have been due to the fact that I was well equipped and able to look after myself, and I always managed to supply them with plenty of game meat. As everywhere in Central Africa, my movements were always well known to villages far ahead and it was rare for me to arrive at any village without receiving from the chief the usual peace offering in the shape of a goat or fowls. This generosity took on a distressing form when I arrived at a village one morning. About an hour after I had pitched camp the chief and two of his followers came to visit me. The old man was most apologetic for not being able to present me with a goat or fowls, but he had done the next best thing, and that was to bring me the freshly killed body of a child. On my marches between villlages I often came across natives carrying their packs on their backs; on the outside of the pack it was not unusual to see tied a human leg or arm.

"I lived amongst these people for nearly two years, and as I have said, I got on very well with them. When I finally decided to quit the country it was not on account of any grievance or fear of them, but because I was led to believe that I could do better farther north, and that was how I eventually landed in the Cameroons and occasionally crossed over the border into Southern Nigeria. I did fairly well there from a trading point of view, but as far as hunting was concerned I found these the most impossible countries in the world. This was not due to the lack of game but to the fact that every living creature, from a rat to an elephant, was in some way or other associated with a ju-ju.

"My first experience in this direction was distinctly unpleasant; on arriving at a large village the chief took me to a big hut which was kept especially for visitors. Like most of the huts in those parts, this one had a very low roof. As I lay reading by the light of a hurricane lamp that night, there was a sudden 'flop' on my mosquito net; closer investigation revealed that the disturbance was due to a six-foot cobra which had fallen from the roof. I quickly got out of bed and killed the snake, after which I started to examine the roof closely. In spite of the poor light I managed to kill six more of these poisonous reptiles with a little .410 shot-gun I carried with me. The shooting soon attracted a crowd, and they were horrified to see so many snakes lying dead on the floor. It was, however, not the fact of there being so many snakes in the place that

10

disturbed them—by having killed the brutes I had seriously offended the snake ju-ju. The snakes, the chief explained, were quite harmless, being controlled by a ju-ju who they pacified daily with prayers and other offerings. A moment later the snakes were all carefully dissected and the gall removed in each case by the medicine man. Snake gall is a very powerful medicine and is used extensively in most of their rites. My indiscriminate slaughter of these 'harmless' creatures inevitably brought more serious repercussions, for the next morning I had to join a number of elders at the ju-ju tree where, like them, I had to pray for forgiveness. This, in itself, was not too bad, but when my cook came to me later in the day with several pieces of snake and explained that the medicine man had ordered him to put these in my food so as to obtain complete forgiveness from the ju-ju, I felt that they were taking things a bit too far.

"Unpleasant as it was, this ju-ju control in so far as snakes were concerned did not worry me too much, but I soon found out that it extended to every other animal in the bush—so much so that I was not allowed to go out hunting without a reliable guide who could read the signs and thus prevent me from committing further indiscretions that would incur the wrath of the different ju-jus—a wrath that would recoil, not only on me, but on the entire community. What it all amounted to was that as long as I was prepared to hunt according to the rules and left the ju-ju protected animals alone, all would be well. Failing this there would be no hunting for me and it would be better if I vacated the district without undue delay.

"These were the conditions that applied when I went out after a herd of six elephants one morning. Within a short time we caught up with them. After a careful survey the guide signalled to me that all was well and I dropped a big bull. The other five elephants, instead of running away or charging, immediately crowded round the fallen beast and started to stroke him with their trunks whilst uttering mournful trumpet-ings. It was the first time I had ever seen elephants behaving in this manner and the thought flashed through my mind that this was more ju-ju business. A moment later a big bull with a pair of magnificent tusks turned round and faced us. I was busy lining him up for a brain shot when he suddenly lifted his front leg. That was a sign that he was ju-ju protected and the guide shouted at me not to shoot. Another bull with fair tusks shook his head violently—that also indicated that he was 'protected'. By this time I began to fear that the elephants might take it into their heads to start a charge and I fired a few shots over their heads to avoid such a possibility. A second later we could hear them thundering through the forest.

"On another occasion we followed a big bull with the finest pair of tusks I ever saw on an elephant. We were close behind him when he walked down the bank of the river, and I made up my mind to shoot as soon as he entered the shallow water in the open. All would have been well if the bull did not stop in midstream and look at the water, for that indicated that he was 'protected' and was at that moment communicating with the water spirit, after which he would descend below water and assume a human shape.

"As I have said before, these severe restrictions applied not only to elephants; they were particularly severe in the case of bush cows and leopards. Those that were not 'protected' could be shot, but in every case the meat had to be taken to the village chief who would retain what he wanted for himself and dis-tribute the rest 'under guidance'.

"But if the ju-jus interfered with my normal hunting, they did make amends in other directions. On the days when we went out and I drew a blank we all gathered under a tree at night and offered sacrifices to the ju-ju who controlled the fortunes of hunters. Invariably I had better luck the next day, which went to prove that the sacrifices had been accepted and the ju-ju was 'on the job'. On the Sanaga River I once saw a most incredible demonstration of blind faith in the powers of the ju-ju. Crocodiles are very numerous and troublesome in this river and frequent appeals are made to the river ju-ju to curb their activities. When I landed on the bank of the river one afternoon a crowd had gathered to watch a big croc in the water. Suddenly one of the men dived into the river and swam towards the brute. In his right hand he had a stout piece of timber about fifteen inches long and seven or eight inches in circumference. Both points were needle sharp and a rope securely tied to the centre. As the man approached the croc he extended the hand in which he held the spiked timber and moved up closer. A moment later the vice-like jaws snapped to over his hand. That was the signal for those who were holding the other end of the rope to go into action. A few minutes later the monster was pulled ashore, the pointed spikes protruding through top and bottom jaws. This was the one and only occasion on which I have ever seen a croc handled in this manner. When I asked the headman what would have happened if there were other crocs in the vicinity or if the one they had accounted for should have snapped from the side and missed the spiked timber, he looked at me as though I had taken leave of my senses and went on to explain that the ju-ju would never permit such a thing to happen.

"Although I spent a great deal of time in the field looking for good tuskers, I never once saw any sign of a lion, and the natives told me there were no lions in those parts. Elephants were quite plentiful and so were the little red Congo buffaloes. Both elephants and buffaloes are extremely dangerous animals if molested, but the one animal these natives fear more than any other is the leopard, and this dread of the leopard, I believe, was responsible for the formation of that most evil secret society —the Leopard Men. During my stay I was introduced to the chief of the society—the most powerful of all secret societies in

West Africa. That they are an evil crowd and responsible for many crimes is quite certain, but in their favour it must be said that they are subject to a central control and crimes of violence are committed only as a result of judgements of the heads of the society. The band of cut-throats and murderers who roam about Central Africa and operate under the name of Leopard Men are in no way associated with this organized secret society.

"During my stay in this country I witnessed, and took part in, many of their strange ceremonies—many of which were quite harmless. One of their strange customs which may appeal to ladies in more civilized parts is that of the 'Fatting House', where a girl betrothed in marriage is kept in seclusion, fed and clothed and all her wants attended to for a period of up to one year. During that time she is not allowed to do any work whatsoever. At the wedding ceremony incisions are made on the right wrists of the contracting parties and each sucks and swallows the blood of the other. If after marriage one of them commits an act of infidelity the blood of the other party will course so rapidly in the veins of the offender that death is sure to result. I am, however, inclined to believe that the theory has been put to the test on many occasions—and found wanting.

"I remained in this country until after the death of the chief of the tribe and was present at the funeral rites. After the body had been washed in warm water and one of the sub-chiefs had taken several mouthfuls of 'ju-ju water' and squirted it over the dead man, the body was lowered into a grave by six men. No women were allowed to attend the ceremony. After burial a wake was commenced which was due to last six months. At the expiration of that time the six men who lowered the body into the grave would be killed and interred in the grave of the chief so that he would not land in the next world without servants to attend his wants. The six men in question were friendly folk and personally known to me, for they had accompanied me on several outings on the trail of elephants, and I did not like facing the ordeal of seeing them killed in this manner, and it was then that I decided to find my way back south and here, as you see, we can hunt in peace without the interference of the ju-ju."

Harry was right. The ju-jus did not interfere with us, but the heat and the close approach of the heavy rains would have been quite as trying, and I decided to get on my way whilst the going was good. A few days later we bade each other adieu and I returned to my headquarters in the Katanga.

15

KILLERS IN ACTION

M Y OBSERVATIONS in the bush have convinced me that, with but few exceptions, such as the rhino, man-eating lions and the croc, there is no animal in the forest that is really dangerous to man in the normal course of events. It is when they are molested, wounded, or suffering from disease or injuries, or when they believe the safety of their young is threatened that they will become aggressive and resort to violence.

Most of the thrilling accounts of encounters with enraged animals have found their origin in such settings, and stories of this type never fail to excite lovers of adventure. This is as it should be, for it is a fact that once the chips are down and an animal makes up its mind to settle the score, the outcome, with very few exceptions, is death to one of the protagonists.

With the perfection of the modern rifle and in most cases a fair amount of experience to support the hunter, the dice are heavily loaded against an aggressive animal, and this explains why there are so many survivors to tell the story of their encounters.

When a man stands with his back to the wall, so to speak, and every second is of vital importance, the mind is concentrated on only one thing—the quickest and most effective manner in which to escape from death or serious injury, and under such conditions there is little, or no time for careful observation of details. This will explain why so few accurate descriptions have ever been given of the characteristics—the *modus operandi* of killer animals in action.

It has been my good—or bad—fortune to be in at a good many kills, quite often as a spectator, and I have often been surprised when reading about, or listening to, stories about famous "last stands", to note how misleading such accounts generally are. In this connection the lion is perhaps the most frequently misrepresented, for in most accounts of the last minutes of an attack he is described as having *jumped* on, or killed his adversary with one stroke of the paw. If this description were applied to the lion's method of attack where other animals are concerned, it would be quite correct, but in the case of human beings it is not so. In the latter case, the lion does not *jump* on his victim, nor does he use his paws to strike. His method of attack on a man facing him is identical with that of a dog, *i.e.* he stands on his hind legs and he grips with his paws, and it is only during the course of the struggle—often in the first few seconds—that the man, being the weaker of the two, is forced down on the ground; and once there, the lion's clumsy and awkward manner of attacking a man often leaves his victim sufficient time to inflict serious, if not fatal, injuries if he has, for example, a knife.

The proof of this assertion is the fact that there are so many well authenticated cases on record where a *corps-à-corps* struggle on the ground has been so protracted that there was time for outside assistance to come to the rescue and change the course of the battle. From my own experience, I can vouch for two cases where fellow-hunters managed to get the better of lions with the use of a knife and a short spear.

On a number of occasions when I have watched lions attack zebras and other animals, the movement has been so rapid that it was not possible to tell from a distance to what extent the paws were used to strike down the prey; so far as I was able to observe, they were used only to grip whilst the serious damage was being inflicted with the fangs, and whereas the lion is astonishingly efficient as a quick killer where animals are concerned, he is comparatively clumsy and awkward in the case of human beings.

In conversations with natives who have either survived or witnessed these man *v.* lion battles, they were all agreed on one point, and that is that the terrifying demonstration of fury a wounded lion stages *before* he starts his attack is one of the most nerve-shattering ordeals in the bush. In this connection an old native hunter who survived one encounter and witnessed two others, put it very succinctly when he told me: "If I had to choose death between a lion and a buffalo, I would prefer the buffalo every time, for he gets on with the business and does it quickly; the lion kills you twice—before he starts on the job, and after he has got you at his mercy."

For my present purpose I have selected three true stories at random which will help to illustrate the lion's lack of finesse when it comes to dealing with human beings. Here is the story of Kabunda, a magnificent, powerfully built six-foot Yao, weighing all of 200 lb., with three fingers, and half of his left hand missing—the result of a man-to-man encounter with our friend Simba:

"This lion had got into the habit of raiding our goat kraals regularly until it got so bad that we put out a nightly watch of six men armed with spears and one gun. It was on a night when I was on duty that he entered the enclosure in which we were sitting under cover waiting for him. There was a half moon which made visibility fairly good, and when he jumped over the fence we were ready for him. I fired one shot at him and all five of the others threw their spears. From the loud grunts the lion made before he got away we felt certain that he was wounded. When the excitement was over we found one goat with three spears sticking in it, another spear was lying on the ground; it had no blood on it which meant that it had missed the mark also.

"Early the next morning we followed the raider's tracks; at

first it was easy, for there was a lot of blood to guide us, but then it started to rain and after a heavy downpour all the tracks were washed away. We spent the whole day looking for the lion but had no luck and gave it up at sunset. The next day also we went out and had no better luck. On the third day only one man accompanied me and after a while we separated, each going in a different direction. After I had walked for nearly an hour I saw a kongoni standing asleep under a tree. I crept up cautiously to it and fired for the shoulder from a short distance. I could hear the bullet strike and saw the kongoni running off at a great speed.The blood trail showed that the animal was bleeding from the lungs and I knew it could not go far. By now I had forgotten all about the lion and that was the reason why I did not look out carefully when I followed the blood spoor into long grass. A few yards ahead of me I saw the kongoni standing with its head down; it looked very sick and I crawled up to it until I was close enough to spear it. It was as I rushed up to the buck to finish it off that I saw the lion a few yards to my right.

"It was a terrifying sight, for the mane was raised, the fangs bared and the ears pulled back, whilst the tail was swinging from side to side. Suddenly he made a terrible roar and then came for me. With my spear gone and the unloaded rifle which I had thrown down, I had only my hunting knife with which to defend myself, but before I could get at it the lion was on top of me. His mouth was wide open and I grabbed his bottom jaw with my left hand whilst with my right hand I got hold of his mane behind his neck. In this way I managed to keep his jaws from my throat whilst we struggled, but the lion was too strong for me and in a short while we were both lying on the ground. I still held on to his jaw with my left hand which was now paining terribly, for the lion had fastened his fangs on to it. As we were rolling on the ground I suddenly remembered my hunting knife which luckily hung on my belt on the right side, and I pulled it from the scabbard. When I drove the knife into its ribs the first time the lion grunted savagely; twice more I lashed out with the knife and each time he grunted louder. After the third stab he stood up straight, shook his body and walked off, but he only walked about five yards when he collapsed.

"I was so tired and shaken that I was unable to get to my feet for some time, but after a little while I felt better and I managed to get up. The lion was quite dead; it must have been the last stab that penetrated to his heart. My hand was in a terrible state and three fingers were hanging on by a bit of skin. I had no medicine with me or bandages; the wound was so painful and bleeding so rapidly that I did not think I would ever get back home, but I managed to reach there shortly before sunset. We luckily had some iodine which we applied to the wounds after we had washed them in hot water. That same night I was carried in a *masheila* to a siding fifty miles from our village, and the next train took me to Dodoma where I received proper medical attention. Apart from the three fingers which I lost, I suffered only a few scratches, but they did not worry me very much.

"I was told afterwards that, apart from the three knife wounds, the lion had a fractured shoulder and a spear wound in his hind leg. These were the wounds he received the night he raided the goat kraal, and had it not been for the loss of the use of his shoulder he would undoubtedly have killed me before I had time to use my knife. The most terrible part of the whole business was the loud roaring in my ears all the time the fight lasted. I never knew that the roar of a lion could be so terrible."

Kabunda's story makes it quite clear that, in his case, the lion did not *jump* on him when he attacked. The fact that it suffered from a fractured shoulder might have been a deterrent, but these conditions did not apply in Mafunza's case. He was not a hunter, nor was he blessed with the physical strength of Kabunda, but he did have the advantage of the assistance of his younger brother, a youth of about eighteen years of age. I leave him to tell his story:

"My brother and I were returning from a village ten miles away where we had attended a wedding and drank plenty of beer; we did not leave for home until after midday and should have reached our village before sunset. In our district we had never had trouble with lions before, although a village near the river fifteen miles away had been raided twice by a man-eater. The men folk managed to beat him off with fires and spears and they suffered no casualties, and as there had been no further sign of the lion we believed that he had left the district. I was walking in front of my brother on a narrow footpath and it was at a sharp bend in the path before it led into long grass where I came face to face with the lion, he was lying in the centre of the narrow path facing in my direction. When I first saw him he was not more than three paces from me, and as soon as he saw me he made a leap for me and jumped on top of me.

"I had nothing with which to defend myself as my spear had been knocked from my hand, and all I could do was to grab the lion round his neck and hold tight whilst he tried to get hold of me by the shoulder with his jaws. My brother was some distance behind me and when he came round the bend he saw me struggling with the lion. Before he could get up to us we both fell to the ground. By this time the lion had sunk his fangs into my shoulder and I was forced to let go my grip round his neck on account of the pain. I cannot remember clearly what happened after that, but my brother luckily carried a heavy *shoka* (native axe), and he attacked the lion with it from the back. The second blow penetrated the skull and entered the brain, and the big head sunk on to my chest after which the lion lay still on top of me. My brother dragged the carcass from me and helped me to get to my feet. Apart from the four holes where the fangs had entered my shoulder, there were no other wounds, not even a scratch. When we examined the lion we found that he was a very old beast; he was so starved that only a few inches separated his stomach from his spine, and his teeth were worn down completely. If that were a young lion with sound teeth he would surely have killed me before my brother arrived on the scene. The only noise he made was a snarl when he jumped on top of me."

Mafunza's undoubtedly was a terrifying experience, but it all happened so suddenly that one might forgive him if his observation and description of the sequence of events is a little faulty. The lion obviously could not have jumped on him in the first place for had it done so he would have been knocked to the ground before he could have grabbed it round its neck and struggle for a short while until they both fell to the ground. However emaciated a lion may be, a full-grown male specimen will always exceed 200 lb. At the very most, Mafunza weighed a paltry 120 lb., and if the lion had jumped on him he would not have remained standing long enough to grab it by the neck.

One of the most fantastic lion stories I ever listened to was that of Bint Lumello, who was the heroine, not only of her own village, but of an area of more than two hundred square miles. Bint was an inhabitant of a village in a district which had suffered severely from the raids of man-eaters. The number of people taken by the brutes was said to exceed forty, which is probably an exaggeration in order to boost the lady's fame. On the day of her famous exploit she was sitting by the fireside at twilight. The men folk of the village were still out in the *bundu* on the trail of the man-eater which had made an unsuccessful attempt to collect a meal from one of the huts the previous night. On the fire before her, and mounted on bricks, a *debbi* (4-gallon petrol tin) of water stood boiling in readiness for the maize meal to be mixed in it on the hunters' return. Here is that part of Bint's story that describes her amazing adventure.

"The *debbi* of water was boiling and the light was beginning to fade when I heard the sound of footsteps on the other side of the fire. I looked up, expecting to see the first of the hunters returning; instead of that I looked into the face of a big lion. He did not make any noise, but when he saw that I was aware of his presence he drew back his ears and started to bare his fangs. I was petrified with fear, for what could I, a feeble woman, do against a big man-eater?

"Suddenly I thought of the boiling water right next to me. I grabbed the tin from the fire and emptied it into the lion's face. That was when he growled savagely and a moment later I saw him trotting off away from me. I rushed to my hut and shut the door quickly. A little while later the hunters returned and I told them all about it. At first they would not believe me, but when they saw the big patch of wet sand and the lion's spoors in the centre of it, they soon prepared big grass flares and followed in the direction the lion had gone. Not long after they had gone we heard loud shouting, and a moment later one of the men came running back to tell us that they had found and killed the lion with their spears.

"When we examined it in the light the next day we found it had been completely blinded by the boiling water, and all the skin on the head was hanging loose like a piece of boiled meat."

This, apparently, was the man-eater that was responsible for all the trouble, for up to the time I passed through the village, which was more than a year after Bint's adventure, there had been no more trouble with lions. Hers was certainly an amazing exploit for a woman and her story also helps to illustrate the fact that lions do not jump at their prey where human beings are concerned. In the present case, nothing would have been easier for the lion than to jump a distance of about three yards and grab the woman before she could lift the tin of boiling water. The fact that he did not proves that it is not their way of attacking man, for if it were, escapes would be very rare indeed. The impact of a 400–500-lb. lion flying through space and landing on a man—whatever his physical strength, would knock all the resistance out of him and might easily result in a fractured spine or neck, and if the lion had a little more *savoir faire* in the matter of handling a human adversary, the list of those who write and tell of how they got the better of the king of beasts in a mortal combat would be greatly reduced.

Another animal whose method of attack is often incorrectly described—especially amongst natives who have survived to tell the story—is the buffalo. Whenever I have listened to narrators of such stories I have always been told that "he came for me with his head down . . ." In the case of buffalo, I have a considerable amount of first-hand personal experience to fall back on, and in over thirty "last ditch stands", I never once saw a buffalo bull charging with his head down. They just do *not* do it that way.

Perhaps not so terrifying as the lion in his preliminary actions, the buffalo, nevertheless, is capable of sending cold chills down the spine of any man facing a determined charge. In long-distance charges—rarely more than seventy-five yards, the action starts by lifting the head high and staring at his foe intently. A shake of the head, a snort, a pawing of the ground, a lifting and swinging of the tail, often accompanied by loud grunts, and down go the chips. The horns are thrown back on the shoulders, the nose points out straight, whilst loud bellowing accompanies the charge throughout. Froth billows from the nostrils, and if you wait for him to approach close enough, you will see two red orbs; they are the eyes in which burn the fires of a fiendish, implacable hatred. If you have waited long enough to take all this in carefully, there is precious little time left to place a heavy bullet in a vital spot, for that will be the only thing to save you from certain death.

On at least two occasions I waited long enough to see those eyes—and a black hulk of 2,000 lb. ploughing up the ground a few feet from me. It is not necessary for me to emphasize the fact that I did not allow these nerve-destroying situations to develop because I was anxious to see what a charging bull's eyes look like at close quarters. On the contrary, on each occasion the brute had rushed through a hail of lead from a heavy calibre rifle and luck came to the rescue at the very last moment.

Vindictive and unforgiving as the buffalo is when his anger is roused, he often allows his intended victim to escape because of his own stupidity. The smallest tree that will sustain the weight of a man beyond the reach of his horns will provide comparative safety, for, unlike the elephant and rhino, it never dawns on a buffalo that a gentle push with his mighty neck and horns will topple both tree and man to the ground and leave him free to carry out his design.

In the case of elephant—amongst the first three of effective killers—there is seldom any marked difference in the description of a charge and there is very little to add to what has been said by others. A debatable point is whether the elephant's awkward habit of pulling his victim to pieces, limb by limb, is due to vindictiveness. In the case of a cow defending a calf it might well be the case, but in general, I do not think the elephant is ever really vindictive in the sense that a bull buffalo is. An old native hunter whose name I have forgotten, probably hit the mark when he explained it to me in this way: "I have often watched a monkey catch a locust. After he has killed it he sits and looks at it for a while and then pulls off the legs, one by one, without any sign of anger. When I sat high up in a tree one morning and watched a big bull elephant kill one of my friends, I saw him walk away from the corpse. After a while he returned, sniffed at the body, then put one big foot on it and pulled off a leg which he threw into the grass beside him; he stood for a while as though in deep thought and then pulled off the other leg and tossed it into the grass. After that he did the same thing with the arms, but he never showed any more anger than the monkey does when he pulls off the legs of the locust, and when it was all over he tore down some branches and covered the remaining piece of the body, after which he started grazing as though nothing had happened."

Of the *modus operandi* of the two lesser killers, the rhino and the leopard, there is also very little disagreement. Unlike the lion, the leopard definitely does jump on his victim. This was often demonstrated to me when I played with those I raised as pets. When the fun was at its best and the excitement rose to a high pitch, they would jump at me from distances of over ten feet, but as it was all done in fun, only my clothes suffered in the process. When they attack in anger it is done in a series of bounces, and they are then the most difficult and dangerous animals to deal with, for they use the claws of both the front and hind feet and the fangs are always directed towards the jugular vein. They are awkward animals to hit when they come at full charge, but against that, they succumb to injury much quicker than a lion.

The rhino never varies in his method of attack. Personally, I do not believe that it is a question of vindictiveness as much as nervousness that prompts a charge during which he is guided by scent far more than by sight. Every foreign smell spells danger to him, and when he thinks his safety is threatened the head goes down, the tail rises, and he thunders along, blowing steam throughout the charge. It needs very little agility to side-step his rush, and once he has passed his objective and lost the scent, he is quite satisfied that all danger is over, after which he will go his way feeding peacefully. My observations in this chapter are based on personal experiences and on reliable first-hand accounts from others. It is, however, well to remember that, whereas animals generally follow a pattern, there are always the exceptions to the rule.

16

INNOCENT VICTIMS

I T WOULD be strange if, during my long sojourn in the bush in different parts of Africa, I did not come across many cases of native cruelty where animals are concerned. In my previous book *African Buffalo Trails* I gave a short account of a big native hunt on the Sira River in Tanganyika in which scores of animals were surrounded by a ring of fire and burnt to death— a procedure which is still adopted in many parts of Central Africa, even today, during the dry season when the grass is ready for burning.

On such occasions the animals have to contend, not only with a fire which effectively cuts off every avenue of escape, but also with hundreds of native hunters armed with spears, bows and arrows, muzzle-loaders, scavenger dogs, and traps which are set at every point where the animals are likely to make a bid for freedom. The only reason why some of the encircled animals do escape on such occasions is because there are so many of them that it is physically impossible for the hunters to destroy them all.

On many occasions I have come across birds with their wings and legs fractured, lying at a marked place where they would be collected later in the day. The reason for this was that the hunters had gone farther afield for more important game and could not be bothered to carry dead weight whilst out hunting. Small antelopes, hares, etc., were also regularly subjected to similar treatment and left to lie in the broiling sun for many hours without water or protection from the heat. This is a common procedure with every native tribe in Central Africa.

In the Rift Valley, whilst I was engaged on locust control work, I once selected an ox to be slaughtered for native food; amongst the native staff there were many Swahilis who will not eat meat unless the throat of the animal is cut in accordance with their religion, and this was what I expected them to do in the present case. A quarter of an hour after I had left them to it my attention was drawn to loud laughing and shouting at the slaughter-house, and I went over to investigate the cause of so much hilarity. On arrival at the scene I found the ox lying on the ground with both its hind legs fractured below the knees. The onlookers were amused by the fact that the ox, apparently of an aggressive temperament, was unable to get at them in its maimed condition—the legs had been all but severed with a heavy axe. They all stood laughing and tantalizing the animal whilst the headman was at his hut, half a mile away, looking for a suitable knife with which to cut the throat. This was one of the very few occasions in the bush when I could not find words to reason with the "gentle African" and resorted to considerable violence on my account. Apparently I carried matters a little too far, for, later in the day, four of the culprits, bearing unmistakable evidence of my outburst, appeared outside my tent and asked to be paid off as they were not prepared to work for a European who will beat people for no reason at all.

From the African's point of view such barbarous crimes are perfectly normal, and they can see no cause for condemnation and justify such acts in this manner: In the first case, that of the fire, they needed the meat—all of it, and they found the most effective manner in which to secure the maximum quantity with a minimum of trouble. In the second case, they secured the birds, but hoped to get bigger game, perhaps many miles away; what sense is there then to carry a lot of dead birds for long distances? In the third case, the ox was aggressive and troublesome and might have escaped whilst they were waiting for the man with the knife, in which case I would not have given them another beast to slaughter and they would have had to go without meat for a whole week.

In each case there was a personal interest at stake and their sole object was to *secure* that interest in the most effective manner. I could go on for hours citing cases of native cruelty in the bush, but this subject has been so completely covered in that recent excellent book *Animal Africa*, written by Mr. Earl Denman, that there is no justification for me to enlarge upon it.

As an ex-hunter, it is quite natural that I do not see eye to eye with the author on every point he raises, but he has marshalled his facts well and his strictures on the biltong and ivory hunters are none too severe. My main objection to this book is that it appeared a little too early; for if the author had waited a few months longer he would have been able to include in his list of crimes the one which I consider the most inhuman of all, and in this case we are not dealing with savages who, in spite of their barbarous cruelty, may plead justification because the driving motive in many cases was hunger. The biltong and ivory hunters likewise have a personal interest which, if it cannot be pleaded as a mitigating circumstance, at least offers an explanation of their crimes; and in their favour it must be said that in many cases they do try to destroy the animals as quickly and humanely as possible. In saying this, I am not pleading, nor am I making excuses for the perpetrators of these crimes which I condemn as strongly as any other thinking person, my object is merely to try and explain the motive behind it all.

But what must we think of a civilized European government which plans deliberately to destroy helpless animals, and knowingly condemns them to suffer for weeks on end before death finally relieves them of their suffering? I refer to the action of the Southern Rhodesian Government in condemning thousands of game animals to a death of thirst in the Zaka area of the Fort Victoria district during the months of August and September, 1957. These are the months of the "dry season" in Southern Rhodesia when water is scarce in the entire district, and in the Zaka area it is obtainable only in the river which flows through it. In this area daily temperatures soar to above 100 degrees, and for centuries past animals by the thousand have depended on the river for their sole water supply. In this year of grace, 1957, they suddenly found that a fence had been erected to cut them off from their only water supply, and in a matter of only two months over a thousand zebras, buffaloes and other game animals were left to perish from thirst on the sun-baked plains of the Fort Victoria district.

This monstrous, inhuman crime was committed on the instructions of a government department on the pretext that it would stop the spread of the tsetse fly in the area. During the years I have myself destroyed hundreds of animals on tsetse control, and whatever may be said for, or against, such a procedure, the fact remains that, in each and every case the animals were destroyed in the quickest and most humane manner possible. That the control of game movements and the destruction of animals under certain circumstances is an effective method of preventing the *spread* of the tsetse fly is not disputed. That such methods are likely to contribute anything towards the *destruction* of the fly is by no means certain. If the authorities in the present case felt that the animals had to be prevented from roaming as far as the river in their search for water, it could hardly have been a snap decision taken on the spur of the moment, and it would be idle to pretend that they could not foresee the results of their action in erecting a fence without first making the necessary arrangements to provide an adequate water supply for the animals.

A similar unavoidable situation arose in South Africa some years ago in the case of the Addo Bush elephants and also in other drought-stricken areas in the Kruger National Park, but the animals were not left to perish from thirst, for the authorities took prompt action to ensure regular water supplies by sinking bore-holes and erecting windmills and troughs where the animals could satiate their thirst. The outlay was by no means prohibitive and it ensured the preservation of thousands of head of game of all species. If for any reason whatever the government in the present case could not make similar arrangements in the Fort Victoria district, a better and more humane method would have been to enlist the services of qualified hunters—of which there are hundreds in Rhodesia—to destroy the animals in a humane manner.

It is gratifying, however, to know that many of the barbarities of the past are no longer practised on such a large scale. In practically every African colony authorities deal severely with those who commit offences against the game laws of the country, and traps and pits are not operated on anything like the scale of earlier times. The ivory and biltong hunter operates on a very much reduced scale, for ivory licences in most countries are so costly and the returns so poor that the game is hardly worth the candle. The indiscriminate shooting of raiders—one of the principal grievances against elephants—has also been curbed to a great extent as in most cases the different game departments take the necessary steps to give relief where it is necessary. And even on tsetse control a more humane outlook prevails. In 1947 a big movement was set afoot to control the borders of Northern Rhodesia and Tanganyika where East Coast fever had broken out. The border had to be patrolled for more than one hundred miles, and instructions were very definite on the point that animals were to be destroyed only in cases of necessity; for the rest, they were to be kept away from the border by ineffective gunfire and noise. This is a great improvement on the old days when "shoot to kill" was the order of the day.

Perhaps the greatest mass destruction of game today occurs in Northern Rhodesia where ten thousand natives, armed with muzzle-loaders, take their daily toll of game animals. In discussing the matter with an official of the Game Department some time ago, I was told that these native hunters each kill on the average four animals per year and wound at least twice that number. At this rate of destruction it is not surprising that, during a stay of over two years, the only animal I ever saw in an area of over two hundred square miles was one duiker.

I agree that hunting is, to a large extent, the only way in which natives in those parts can obtain an occasional supply of meat and that they are entitled to some consideration in this respect. But I know also that hundreds of them are not fit and proper persons to be left at large with fire-arms—especially of such an inferior nature that, in the process of hunting, four out of every five animals are not killed, but wounded and left to the mercy of carnivorae, or die in misery and pain as a result of their wounds. The average native will not waste much time to track down a wounded animal, for he is completely devoid of any sporting or humane sense in such matters and he cannot see the wisdom of following a wounded animal for miles, sometimes without success, when a few hundred yards from where he made his last unsuccessful attempt another animal may offer itself as a target.

In the Lake Katavi area in Tanganyika some years ago, buffalo hunting was as hazardous an occupation as one could find anywhere. Buffaloes are particularly numerous in that part of the country—and so are the native hunters with their antiquated old muzzle-loaders. There have been so many fatal accidents with buffalo in that district that it is extremely rare for a native hunter to try and trail a wounded animal. During the eighteen months I hunted in this area I had more unpleasant incidents with buffaloes than I had during the preceding eighteen years in other parts of Africa, and this was due entirely to the fact that so many of these animals were left at large with pieces of lead and scrap iron in their hides. The only redeeming feature in the Katavi area is the grim consolation that many of the wounded buffaloes are successful in settling their grievances with their tormentors, for during the first twelve months I spent in this district, a dozen fatal accidents were reported amongst native hunters. As may be expected, the natives in those parts look upon the buffalo as the most wicked and dangerous animal on earth, and not one of them has a good word to say for "Mbogo".

17

THOSE WHO SURVIVED

O NE OF the most fascinating and admirable traits of the raw
native in the back blocks is his reticence to speak of his past
experiences in the bush—especially when they pertain to
narrow escapes from death.

In these days of rapid travel, which enables a man to leave
New York or London by air for Nairobi, spend ten days on a
guided safari and be back in his office just a fortnight later,
many outdoor magazines that cater for adventure stories have
stock-piles to draw from for a century or two. Quite recently I
have read several breathtaking stories in which the writers told
of their daring adventures in "darkest Africa". One six-page
article told of a successful hunt of an eland bull which lasted
several days and gave a graphic account of how the "monarch
of the valley" was eventually "slain". Others told of hair-
raising adventures with such dangerous animals as zebra,
kongoni, etc., which were also "slain" in the end.

When reading some of the best of these stories by the modern
"fortnighters" one cannot help but feel that men like Selous,
Norton, and Bell were mere novices at the hunting game. How
different all this is when compared with the modesty and
reticence of the raw African who spends his entire life amongst
dangerous animals and considers himself lucky to be in possession of an antiquated old muzzle-loader when facing up to
lions, elephants, buffaloes, etc., whilst out hunting for his daily
food. The African native never hunts for sport.

In the presence of a European whom they do not know very

well, it is extremely difficult to get good native hunters to talk about their narrow escapes and experiences with dangerous animals, and whenever I have been able to persuade them to do so, their accounts have always erred on the side of modesty and with no intention of drawing attention to themselves. Often they have shown me terrible scars received during such encounters, in a most casual manner as though it was the most normal thing to have happened to them in the circumstances.

It has often happened to me to have natives on safari who were completely silent around the camp-fire at night when I sat amongst them and listened to some "old stager" telling of his adventures. A night or two later, when feeling tired or not disposed to join in the camp-fire talks, I have lain on my bed and listened to these men of silence tell the most fantastic—and true—stories of their adventures in the bush. These discussions generally became acrimonious to the extreme when members of different tribes questioned their veracity, and arguments would rage far into the night. It was during these protracted discussions in the white heat of contention that I listened to some amazing stories which I forthwith entered in my diaries, and some of these, I hope, will prove of as much interest to my readers as they did to me.

Chimbandi was a native from a Congo village on the Lualaba River, where crocs were not only numerous but also a dangerous pest. That evening the topic of conversation around the camp-fire was on the subject of crocodiles, for earlier in the day I had shot an outsize specimen on a sand-bank near the river. One of the porters had rushed up after the brute had ceased struggling in its attempt to regain the water. Believing the croc was dead, he had walked up to it and driven a spear into its side; the croc suddenly came back to life and retaliated by making a last dying effort to get at its tormentor, and the monster jaws had actually grazed the leg of the native as they snapped to. An event such as this generally provides excellent material for discussion and in due course one story followed another on the subject of croc depredations.

Black, my old gun-bearer, had just finished telling one of his favourite stories in which he described how he had taken cover behind a big rock near a deep pool of water in the Chambezi River in Northern Rhodesia. The pool was popular with all kinds of game, and it was after 4 p.m., the hour when Mpala groups generally came to quench their thirst and Black was keeping a sharp look-out for something worth while for the pot. At the time he was not hunting with a European and the only weapon he had was an old muzzle-loader which had proved effective on smaller game when shooting across the pool. On this afternoon as he sat waiting for the Mpala, a big elephant bull had put in an appearance on the far side and started drinking. Black was sitting, weighing up the prospects of placing a brain shot, when there was a loud commotion in the water and the bull set up a loud squeal. A moment later the enraged bull dragged a huge croc from the river, hoisted it high up in the air and smashed it down on the ground. Twice more the performance was repeated and the croc lay still without a sign of life. The bull, however, was not quite satisfied with his handiwork and started to dance an the lifeless body of his enemy with his front feet. In a few minutes the croc was flattened out like a piece of paper and the bull returned to the water, quenched its thirst and walked off as though nothing unusual had happened.

The story, as usual, was well received, and it was as his listeners sat turning things over in their minds that Chimbandi broke the silence: "Of all the animals in the bush, the croc is by far the worst. It is a pity that we have not the strength of an elephant, for in that case I would not have fared so badly that morning when I had trouble with one of those big lizards. I was sitting next to a running stream, washing myself, when I was suddenly grabbed by the leg. I tried desperately to free myself, but it was of no use for no man has the strength to escape the grip of one of those devils. A moment later I was pulled under the water where I continued to struggle until I lost consciousness.

"When I woke up again I found myself lying in a dense reed bed; I was so weak that I could not move anything else but my eyes. This, perhaps, was very lucky for me, for when my eyes became stronger and I was able to notice things, I saw the croc lying next to me. It was the most awful thing that has ever happened to me; my leg was paining terribly and every part of my body was aching. I was afraid to move for fear the big devil would grab me again and pull me under water; whilst I lay there in agony I could not tell whether my arms and legs were broken. The reeds were so dense I could not see the sun and I could not tell what time of the day it was—or how long I had been there; for all I knew it might have been for days, for I knew that a croc does not like fresh meat and waits for it to smell before he eats it.

"I was lying there wondering what was going to happen to me when the croc suddenly moved; it crawled round me slowly, came to my side again and looked at me intently for a while; I felt quite certain that it was going to start and pull me to pieces and eat me, but I made up my mind to lie still and see what would happen. Just then the croc turned round quickly and made off for the water, where it disappeared. I quickly kicked out my legs and moved my arms and found that no bones were broken. I did not know how long it would be before the brute would return but I made up my mind to try and get away as quickly as possible. The reeds were too dense for me to get on my feet and run, so I crawled out on my hands and knees as fast as I could. After I had crawled about thirty yards I came to a dry bank and tried to get to my feet, but I was not able to do so as my legs ached too much. I continued to crawl as far as I could from the river bank and shouted loudly all the time for help. After a while I could hear voices, and a little later my friends from the village found me and took me back home. It was not midday yet, so I could not have been lying in the reeds for much more than an hour, but to me it seemed like a year. It was nearly a month before I was able to walk properly and the sores were all healed."

Chimbandi's story was not too well received and several of his listeners expressed their disbelief. By this time I had left my bed and joined the others at the fireside.

"If your story is true and the croc really pulled you under the water, how does it come that you have no marks to show where he fastened his teeth in your leg?" queried Black.

At the beginning of his story Chimbandi did not explain that the croc had seized him by the upper part of his leg. To satisfy Black and any others who might doubt his story, he let down his trousers and exposed his leg to us. I counted nine horrible scars—there could be no possible doubt, they were the imprints of a crocodile's jaws. That was the story of Chimbandi—one of the silent men.

Pindula was another lucky survivor who had an amazing story to tell on another occasion. He, unlike most others who are taken when walking through, or approaching too close to a river, was actually pulled out of a native canoe. Pindula put up a terrific struggle, during which he managed to unsheathe his hunting knife and proceeded to dig it into the saurian's eyes, completely blinding it. This treatment proved too rough, even for a croc, and the brute released its grip and disappeared under the water. The result of this encounter left Pindula with a partly withered arm and numerous scars to bear witness to his narrow escape.

It has always puzzled me to see that natives who will go into a panic of fear at the very mention of a man-eating lion in their district will yet lay themselves open to attack by crocs—the most merciless, and by far the greatest killer of them all—for it is quite certain that crocs claim more victims annually than all the buffaloes, lions and elephants put together. It is not an unusual thing to find men, both white and black, who have been lucky to escape from the last-named animals; to escape from the jaws of a croc, in view of their construction, is very little short of a miracle. With over sixty teeth, the majority of which are in the bottom jaw and fit into cavities of the upper jaw, the croc's grip is a veritable lock which relieves him of all further effort to hang on to his prey. In this manner he is able to use his entire weight in a struggle which already favours him in that it takes place under water as a rule where the brutes can live for an hour or more without surfacing—a feat beyond any of his victims. The strength of a full-grown specimen of twenty feet is something quite unbelievable and has proved more than a match for the largest of buffaloes. Elephants, hippos and rhinos are the only animals capable of putting up a successful resistance against such monsters.

In recent times there has been a brisk trade in croc hides, and as a result of the activities of hunters all over Central Africa their numbers have been reduced to some extent in a few of the larger rivers. But when one considers that a female lays anything up to sixty eggs per year, that she has a probable life span of fifty years and that their only enemies are man and the monitor lizard who devours the eggs, there is no great dangers that their numbers will ever be seriously depleted. In the Lake Kyoga area some thirty thousand were killed in one year—1945—for their skins, and even this did not have any noticeable effect on their numbers. Night shooting so far seems to have proved the best method of hunting the croc, as traps and poison have not given satisfactory results. Poisons like arsenic, strychnine and cyanide are most effective when used against other animals but have little or no effect on the croco-dile for it is speedily ejected.

Whatever profits there may be in crocodile hunting are, to

my mind, completely offset by the hard and unpleasant conditions that attend such an enterprise. To sit in an open motorboat at night—often in pouring rain, in mosquito-infested rivers, is not the easiest way in which to earn money. Shortly before my departure for Europe, a young man came to me in Northern Rhodesia one morning with a proposition that I should finance a six months' hunt. He was full of confidence in such a venture, and went on to explain that he was doing very well on the Zambezi River until the night when a hippo capsized his boat with all the occupants in a croc infested part of the river. Two natives were drowned or seized by the crocs, the boat, his rifle and all his equipment was lost, and he had a miraculous escape from death himself. When the relatives and friends of the two native victims heard about the disaster they turned hostile towards the European whom they held responsible for the accident and he was lucky to escape a second time.

For all that, he felt confident that he could do well if I would help him to replace his lost equipment so as to be able to start afresh. I reluctantly turned down the proposition, for I could not help thinking that his courage by far outweighed his intelligence.

Hunting crocodiles for sport in the ordinary way provides very little excitement, for shooting them on the banks of a river seldom yields returns. Invariably they will make for water, and I am not sure that even a brain shot is always effective, for I have scored dozens of head shots with heavy calibre rifles, only to see the brutes slide into the water where they are very seldom if ever recovered. Perhaps Black had it right when he said it was of no use to shoot for a croc's brain because it had none; the better way was to try and fracture the spine.

18

OTHER SURVIVORS

In parts of the country where lions, buffaloes, elephants and rhinos are to be found in the same district, it has often surprised me to find that natives generally are far more afraid of the rhino than they are of the three other species. This fear of the rhino is probably due to the fact that he is without doubt the most impetuous animal in the bush—a trait which, fortunately, does not make him the most dangerous, or even a very dangerous, animal to contend with.

Natives very rarely take the trouble to observe and analyse animal behaviour correctly. The fact that a rhino will charge a man—or a convoy of men—without direct provocation, stamps him as an aggressive, vindictive animal to be avoided at all costs. This, I feel certain, is a completely wrong analysis of the rhino's character, and I firmly believe that nine out of every ten charges by rhinos have nothing to do with vindictiveness, but are due to extreme nervousness which, in turn, is due to the animal's defective sight and keen senses of smell and hearing.

Under the most favourable circumstances the rhino's sight is limited to about twenty-five yards, whereas his scenting is effective over distances of more than two hundred yards. Most other animals can easily define any object at that distance, and in case of danger they will resort to flight as quickly as possible. The rhino, being seriously handicapped in the matter of sight, reasons quite differently. Since he cannot see well enough to escape from danger, he decides that the best thing to do is to overcome it in the quickest and most effective manner possible, and for this purpose he is better equipped than most other animals—witness the formidable horn, the enormous strength and weight, the protective covering in the shape of an almost impenetrable hide and his natural resistance and indifference to injury. All these assets can be better employed in offence than in defence, hence the many unprovoked charges, which do not signify vindictiveness as much as an anxiety to overcome the threatening danger.

Of the many stories of rhino charges I have listened to— especially in cases of convoys on the move, I can remember only one or two that have ended badly. Msindu's was one, and even in his case a little prudence would have helped to avert the trouble. Here is the story Msindu told us round the camp-fire one night when the topic of conversation was the rhino:

"My uncle and I were the only ones in our village who possessed guns with which to hunt big game. While out hunting one morning we came across a rhino cow with her calf which was about half grown. We decided to shoot the calf because it is difficult to kill a full-grown rhino with the kind of guns we had. We crept up close to the two rhinos, making sure to keep under the best cover there was; when we got within thirty yards of the animals we both fired at the calf and it dropped. The wind must have turned suddenly, for the cow came straight for us in full charge. We did not have time to reload so we both started to run for the nearest tree; before we got half-way to it she caught me from behind and tossed me so high that when I fell on the ground I was several yards behind her as she kept running after my uncle. A moment later I saw his body flying in the air whilst the cow kept running in a straight line for a few yards; then she turned round and again attacked the body and tossed it high in the air. All the time she kept on squealing and blowing off steam. When the body landed on the ground again she walked up to it and sniffed at it for a little while, but

apart from that she did not molest it again. I knew my uncle
was dead and we found afterwards that the horn had penetrated
his lungs and stomach. I was very badly injured in my leg
where the horn had entered and I knew I would never be able
to move fast enough to reach safety, so I lay still and prayed
that she would forget about me after she was satisfied that my
uncle was dead. A few minutes later she started to walk in my
direction; I felt certain that she was coming to kill me too, but
she passed about ten yards from me without noticing me. I
watched her until she disappeared in the bush and then
struggled to a tree, which I mounted. The cow kept on walking
in a straight line and did not go back to her calf again. I
remained in the tree until late in the afternoon when men from
the village found me. They collected the meat of the calf and
carried me back home. I was laid up for a very long time before
my leg began to heal. You can see by this scar what a terrible
wound it was."

Msindu's story confirms what I have said earlier in this
chapter. The attack on his uncle, under the circumstances, was
a most natural and normal thing; that she did not return to
her first victim after she had settled her score with the second
may be due to the fact that she had lost both sight and scent
of him. It is, however, significant that, after she had killed the
other man, the body was not subjected to the kind of mutilation
it would have received from either an elephant, lion or buffalo.

The story of Kasembe, a Northern Rhodesia hunter of the
Mwemba tribe, is a case in point. The setting is almost identical
to that of Msindu's, but the buffalo's method of procedure
once he had his victim at his mercy was very different and
typical of the animal's ferocity and vindictiveness. Kasembe
was another "man of silence" who lived to tell of a most
amazing buffalo escape, and unlike others who had scars to
show in support of their stories, his only proof was a bad limp
in his right leg, which was several inches shorter than the left

—having set badly after it was broken in his encounter with the buffalo. Here is Kasembe's story:

"People who hunt the buffalo should always remember that he is the most cunning and vicious animal in the bush. The morning I went out with a friend to hunt we had only one gun between us and several spears, for we expected to find antelopes near the water pool. Instead we spotted a buffalo bull lying sleeping under a tree. We crept within twenty yards of him when my friend fired for the neck. When the bullet struck him the head went down and we waited for a few moments. There was no further move and, thinking that the bull was dead, we walked up to it. I threw a spear into its side and still there was no move; then my friend also threw a spear into its neck.

"The moment it struck him, the bull came to life, and before he could get to his feet we started to run for the tree from which we had fired the shot, but we had only gone a few yards when we could hear him coming behind us; he was grunting and bellowing loudly. The next instant I received a terrific bump from the side and immediately after that I found myself flying into space, for after the bull had bumped me he had hooked his horn in my trousers leg and tossed me a long way to his side. He took no further notice of me but went after my friend who was still running at top speed. It was open country and I could see everything from where I lay. When that big brute caught up with my friend he hooked him from the side and tossed him so high that when the body came down it landed on the horns and he was tossed a second time. I had no doubt my friend was dead and I knew the buffalo would come back to attack me after he had finished with the other man, so I tried to get up and run for a small tree nearby, but I found my right leg was broken below the hip and all I could do was to crawl up to the tree. All this time I could hear the buffalo grunting and bellowing savagely, and when I looked round I could see him goring and stamping on the body of my friend.

"At last I reached the tree, which was so small I did not think it would support my weight, but after a terrible struggle I managed to get on to a branch not much more than six feet from the ground. The bull was still busy trampling the corpse into the ground and seemed to have forgotten all about me; but a minute later he came trotting towards me and came to a stop when he reached the tree. It was a terrible thing to see him standing there with his horns only a foot or two below me, grunting and bellowing as he stood swinging his head from side to side whilst froth came from his nostrils.

"The pain in my leg was so bad that I began to feel faint and I knew it would not be long before I would fall to the ground. But I luckily had my hunting knife in my belt and I quickly cut my trousers from my body and tore long strips with which I tied myself to the tree trunk. I do not know how many times I lost consciousness that day, but each time I came to I saw the bull walking in circles round the tree. Later in the day he walked over to the corpse of the other man and again pushed it about with his horns. It was only a few minutes before sunset when he walked off into the bush and that was the last I saw of him. By this time I was suffering so much pain I could not remain in the tree any longer, so I loosened the strips and tried to climb down, but everything went black and when I awakened again I found myself lying on the ground, the stars were shining and there was a half moon in the sky. If the bull had returned then there would have been no hope for me, for I had not the strength and suffered too much pain to try and climb that tree again.

"All night long as I lay next to the tree I could hear hyenas calling in the distance, and I feared that if I should go off into a dead faint again they would tear me to pieces. Twice during the night they came very close to me but when I waved my arms they ran away. At the spot where the body of my friend lay there was a terrifying noise for a long time; the hyenas had

found him and I knew they were eating him. That night was
the most terrible one I have ever spent in my life. It was not
only the pain and the fear of being eaten by the hyenas or other
wild animals that worried me; there was the thought that the
bull would come back and find me on the ground. And perhaps
the worst of all was the terrible thirst I was suffering, for my
throat was dry and my tongue was thick in my mouth.

"All the next day I lay beside the tree, moaning and groaning, I was too weak to shout for help, and I began to think
perhaps it would be better if the bull came back and killed me
quickly. I went off into a faint again and after a long time I was
awakened when I felt something licking my face. I got a great
shock for I thought it was a hyena, but when I opened my eyes
I saw that it was a dog from our village. I knew then that the
people from the village had come out to look for us and that
help would soon come to me. A little while later they found me
and gave me water to drink; by that time I was so weak I could
hardly swallow it. When the men went to look for the corpse
of my friend they found only a few pieces of bone; the hyenas
had eaten the rest during the night.

"I was carried back home, where the medicine man put my
leg in splints and gave me medicine to drink. I was laid up for
nearly a year before I could start to walk on crutches; but my
leg set badly, as you can see—it is much shorter than the other.
For all that, I am lucky to be alive. If the bull had hooked my
body instead of my trousers I would not be here now, and the
hyenas also might easily have killed and eaten me that night.

"The next day the hunters from the village went out to look
for the buffalo but they never found a trace of him again. If
we had been a bit wiser that day and thrown our spears into
his heart all might have been well, but he was only stunned by
the bullet and throwing spears at his neck was the worst thing
we could have done."

Whether a buffalo bull is more dangerous to hunt than a

lion or an elephant is essentially a matter of opinion, but I do not think there is any question about his being the most vindictive of all animals in the bush. In this respect the honour— whatever it may be worth, belongs to the male species only, In my own experience I have found that cow elephants and lionesses are more dangerous than the males of their species; in the case of buffaloes it is not so. That a cow will put up a fight in defence of her calf or if she is badly wounded, is quite certain, but the grievance is never carried to the same lengths as in the case of the two other species of females.

The amusing experience of my old gun-bearer, Black, will serve as an illustration. On this occasion I had sent him out with a light sporting rifle to try and find something for the pot. Shortly after leaving camp he found two buffalo cows grazing by themselves. Selecting the larger of the two, he aimed for the head and the cow dropped on receiving the bullet. Believing that he had placed a brain shot, Black walked up boldly, but when he had approached within five yards of the cow she suddenly revived and charged him. Black was much too close to try another shot and immediately took to his heels at high speed. For a little distance he ran in a zigzag course which must have puzzled the cow to the extent of reducing her speed, but a few moments later he found himself completely winded and he decided that the best thing to do would be to face the enemy. To this end, he came to an abrupt stop, turned round and started to wave the rifle at the cow, who must have been taken aback completely by such strange behaviour, for she also came to a stop and stood looking at him intently.

"I did not know what to do next," he told me, "so I started to grunt and bellow loudly just like a bull would do; she looked at me a while longer and then turned and walked off. I was so shaken by the shock of it all that I forgot to shoot at her when she had her back turned to me. It was only after she had disappeared in the long grass that I remembered the gun in my hands, but I decided it would be best to leave her alone for fear there might be more serious trouble for me if she changed her mind."

A cow elephant or a lioness would have handled this situation very differently. It is also possible that Black had a charmed life where buffaloes were concerned, for this was his third successful escape. His story, at all events, was quite true as it was vouched for by two porters who accompanied him and found safety in the tree-tops whilst Black was stepping it out. In addition, the torn and tattered condition of his clothes indicated that he had travelled through a patch of thorn bush at high speed.

19

THE LAST CAMP-FIRE

F ITALI WAS another "man of silence" who I employed on my safari in the Lake Bangweulu district of Northern Rhodesia. He was engaged in the capacity of guide because of his intimate knowledge of the country.

The main attractions at Lake Bangweulu at the time of my safari were otters, Sititunga antelopes and Lechwe antelopes. Otters were especially numerous in the lake district, and their skins, after curing, were fairly valuable. I soon found out that hunting in that part of the world required a technique and organization very different from that employed in other parts of Central Africa. The otter hunters operated mainly at night with spears and nets. The Sititunga there, as in other parts where they are to be found, frequented the dense reed beds in the swamps and had to be hunted in canoes. Lechwe, both red and black, were plentiful, but extremely wary owing to the fact that the natives employed packs of trained dogs to hunt them.

It became obvious to me at an early stage that the financial success of the safari would depend more on trading and bartering than on hunting in the accepted sense. I was determined, however, to bag a good specimen of Sititunga, and when I finally secured one after a week of fruitless effort, I decided to try my luck at ivory hunting, and this was how Fitali came to be a member of my safari.

The resulting elephant hunt helped to compensate for the disappointment at the lake, but the details are not of great importance. For the moment we are concerned with nights around the camp-fires.

That day, as on the two preceding days, we had walked a full twenty miles on the trail of an elephant herd which included an enormous bull if the size of his tracks was anything to judge by. As the sun was about to dip behind the mountains at five o'clock that afternoon, we decided to camp for the night near a fresh-water spring. The nearest we had got to the herd that day was when one of the spotters had heard the rumbling of their stomachs in dense forest, and this was followed by a crashing of branches and trees when the herd picked up our scent. The outlook at the time of pitching camp was pretty gloomy, for during the three days of trailing I had refused to shoot for the pot for fear of putting the elephants on the run. The last of our meat supplies had been consumed the previous night and we were preparing to settle down to "iron rations" which consisted of maize meal, when one of the spotters came rushing in to tell me that he had just seen a herd of eland grazing quite close to camp. In less than an hour the atmosphere of gloom was dispelled and the porters were busy bringing in the meat of a big eland bull which I had bagged without any difficulty. That night the camp-fire burned brightly and the subject of discussion was elephants and their uncanny way of scenting danger. Fitali, who had been sitting listening to the different opinions being expressed, now joined issue:

"It is not only when there are human beings about that they are so quick in scenting danger," he said; "when there are calves in a herd the cows are always on the look-out for any other animals that may harm their little ones. Lions, leopards and hyenas all take great care to keep well out of the way of the cows when the calves are very young. One of the strangest and most unfortunate things that ever happened to our hunting community at the lake was when we left in a party of six one morning to hunt for food. Between us we had four guns, a number of spears and bows and arrows. After we had walked for an hour or so we put up a lion in a patch of grass a few yards ahead of us. It was in fairly open country and as soon as he broke cover all four of us fired at him. At least one bullet hit the mark, for he roared loudly as he leaped in the air and ran off with his hind leg trailing.

"We followed the blood trail in open country for more than two miles until it entered a patch of close scrub. That kind of country is much too dangerous to follow a wounded lion, so we decided to have a council of war before entering close forest. As we stood talking, there was a dead silence all round us; then suddenly we heard branches moving in the trees near us. As we looked in the direction of the sound we saw an elephant cow walking at a fast pace with her trunk extended; behind her there were several other cows and calves, but they were not worrying about us at all even though we had poor cover.

"We were still watching the procession and wondering what it was all about, when the cow in the lead set up a loud squealing and this was followed immediately by vicious snarling and grunting. The other cows all rushed to the spot from where the noise came, and we also moved up in that direction, for we realized that the elephants had found the lion we were looking for. A moment later we could hear branches and trees crashing all over the place. We remained under cover listening to the disturbance until we could hear the grunting and trumpeting receding in the forest. We quickly followed in the trail of the noise, and when we reached the far side of the bush we saw five cows running behind the lion who was making for more wooded country a mile away. Behind the cows followed a big bull, but he was trotting slowly and the calves were running at his sides. The cows were so close on the heels of the lion that we expected them to catch up with him before he would reach the dense scrub, but he just managed to make it in time.

"Although it was a very dangerous thing to do, we decided

to follow up and see what would happen if the lion should be caught. When we came near the edge of the scrub we took cover behind a large bush, where we sat for more than an hour and listened to trees and branches crashing all over the place. After it was all over, the troop came out into the open and started walking in the direction where they had found the lion earlier. We waited until they had gone a safe distance and then went in to examine the place they had just vacated. There we found they had uprooted every bush that could have provided any cover for the lion and several trees were also pushed over, but there was no sign of the lion. Later on we found that he had passed through the dense undergrowth and made for forest country farther ahead.

"After all the excitement was over we had a further discussion and we decided to split up. Three of our men went after the elephants to try and get the bull, for he had very good tusks; the two others accompanied me on the trail of the lion. The blood spoor we had found showed that he was bleeding from the lungs and we knew he could not last very long. We followed the trail until it entered another patch of forest country. These clumps of trees are not very large, so we decided to walk round this one and find out whether the lion had passed through it. My two companions went to the left whilst I went to the right.

"I had not walked more than a hundred yards when I noticed a movement in the grass; a second later I saw the lion walking slowly with his head down. He looked very sick to me and, as the distance separating us did not exceed sixty yards, I felt certain I could knock it over at such short range. I fired for the shoulder and when the bullet struck home the lion grunted loudly and turned round to look at me. I could see there was trouble brewing when he pulled his ears back; when he started to swing his tail I ran for the nearest tree and climbed up it at top speed, but I had only climbed a few feet when I realized that the tree was not big enough to save me. By this time the lion stood snarling beneath me. Suddenly he jumped and lashed out at me with his front paw. I could feel the pain in my leg as he struck me. By now he was roaring and snarling so loudly the tree and the earth seemed to be shaking; and then he made another leap, but he just missed me and that seemed to make him quite mad and he made yet another leap at me. This time he caught my foot in his jaw and I knew it was the end when I started to lose my grip of the tree as he pulled me down. Just as I began falling down I heard a shot, and the next moment I found myself lying on the ground beside the lion, but he was quite dead, only his hind leg moved as he kicked out helplessly.

"While I was in the tree trying to avoid the lion I was so frightened I forgot all about my companions and never expected any help from that source, but they had heard me firing the shot and immediately rushed over to see what it was all about. When they heard the lion grunting and snarling they knew there was serious trouble for me and they crawled up from the side until they were only a few paces from the tree. My friend took careful aim for the neck, but the bullet entered the brain and the lion fell down dead.

"My leg was very badly scratched on the side and there were two deep fang marks in my foot, but I was lucky that the lion did not kill me before my friend came to the rescue. That was the worst thing that has ever happened to me in the bush. I tried to walk back home but the pain was too great, and the other man then went back to the village to bring help. I was carried back to the village and we did not arrive there until sunset; there we were told that the men who had followed the elephants had not returned. We were not very worried about it, for elephants are very difficult animals to hunt when they are on the move. It was near midnight when the hunters returned and brought us the news of the terrible accident they had had with the bull—one of them carried the arm of Alfons which the elephant had torn from his body.

"It was a great mistake for them to go after the elephants that day after the excitement with the lion. When they left us that morning they walked until nearly midday before they found the herd standing sleeping under some trees. At first they could not see the bull, but Bawala circled round the herd by himself and a few minutes later the others heard a shot. This was followed by loud squealing and shouting. Under such conditions one has to be very careful, for the cows are very bad tempered when there are calves about, and if one wounds the bull the rest of the herd will immediately charge. For this reason the other two men lost some time before they could get to the scene of the shooting; there they saw the bull kneeling on the ground whilst Bawala was lying under its stomach, holding on to one of its hind legs. It would have been easy for Alfons to fire a shot into the elephant's brain, as he was only ten yards away, but he did not do that for fear the elephant would fall on top of Bawala and crush him to death. A second later the elephant stood up and pulled Bawala from under him with his trunk; it was as he stood swinging him in the air that Alfons fired for the brain. The bullet did not even stun the bull, and after he had tossed Bawala to the side he rushed after Alfons who was running away. But he did not get far before the bull caught him and pushed one of his tusks through his body. After that he lifted him on his trunk and smashed him down on the ground. When he saw that Alfons was dead he trampled on his body and pulled him to pieces. Bawala was not injured at all and he and the other man managed to get away after they saw that the bull had killed Alfons. Several hours later they went back to the spot. The elephants had gone away and the only part of Alfons's body that was not flattened out was his arm which they brought back with them."

A fortnight later we returned to the lake to collect the otter skins I had agreed to purchase from the village headman. During the course of our safari we caught up with the herd we were trailing on the night Fitali told me his story. The bull was an enormous fellow but his tusks were by no means exceptional. The left one, in fact, was nearly a foot shorter than the other— it had apparently been broken in a fight with other bulls or it could have been shot away.

Whilst we were waiting to trade more otter skins with hunters at the lake, Bawala, the hero of Fitali's story, appeared at my camp one morning; he repeated the story I had heard from Fitali and also gave me some more details as to what had happened on that fateful day, and how he came to be lying under the elephant's stomach when Alfons appeared on the scene. It appeared that the bull had charged him immediately it received the bullet. Bawala had run at top speed with the elephant in hot pursuit. During his flight his foot had hooked in the undergrowth and he went sprawling on the ground. The bull had lowered its tusks to gore him but had missed him by a fraction of an inch and drove its tusks into the ground beside him. It was after he had crawled under the bull's stomach and grabbed it by the hind leg that Alfons appeared on the scene and fired at the elephant when it stood swinging Bawala in the air—a shot that saved Bawala's life but cost Alfons his own.

Fitali had the scars on his leg to show where the lion had clawed and bitten him, but Bawala had not a mark to show for his terrifying experience. Which of them had had the narrowest escape from death that day is anyone's guess, but for a nerve-wrecking experience I am inclined to pick Fitali. Had not the old native hunter said: "The lion kills you twice—once before he starts on the job, and again when he has you at his mercy." That probably is the reason why the lion always figures at the top of the list when dangerous animals are discussed around the camp-fires at night.

After Bawala had left me he went over to the other members

of my hunting staff who were busy dressing skins. There he was shown the tusks of the bull I had shot on my trip. A few minutes later he came rushing back to tell me that the tusks were those of the bull that had killed Alfons; he knew them because of the one which had the point missing. I felt sceptical about it then as I do now—for there are many elephant bulls walking about with parts of their tusks missing. These accidents are common in places where native hunters operate with muzzle-loaders, and fights between bulls also end up in the partial loss of a tusk sometimes. Bawala, however, was firmly convinced that they belonged to the bull that had held him in its trunk that morning. Perhaps he was right; I would not know.

I remained at the lake another fortnight and around the camp-fire one night I listened to the story of two man-eating leopards at the village of the headman. In one case a leopard had killed and eaten no fewer than seven piccaninnies who were herding goats. On occasion it would vary its diet by taking a goat. In another case a leopard had killed a woman by tearing out her throat and eating the body. In both cases the leopards were old and emaciated, which may explain their strange behaviour. As I have mentioned elsewhere, it is extremely rare for a leopard to attack human beings for food; that they will attack when provoked there is no doubt, for they are more sensitive to injury than any other animal I know of. In cases where they have turned man-eater the causes would not be difficult to find—the story is always the same—illness, old age or wounds that prevent them from catching their prey in the normal manner, and even at that, I find that, of all the hundreds of stories I have listened to around the camp-fires at night there was not one about leopards of sufficient interest to include in my memoirs of camp-fire stories.

The camp-fires of memory will burn for ever,
Their fuel the voices telling of the day.